AF507371

My Father is My Little Boy

A Daughter Steps Into Her Father's Alzheimer's World

Nancy Lopez

FIND YOUR VOICE PUBLISHING

Contents

PREFACE

I've changed most names to protect privacy.

In this book I make references to many songs — mostly Spanish songs. I would have liked to include the lyrics but was limited by copyright laws. Rightly so, as anyone who composes a song that passes the test of time should be duly compensated.

If you are anything like me you would want to hear the songs, find the lyrics and even find translations to the songs. The great thing is that in this day and age, you can do all these things on the internet. I encourage you to do so and experience the beauty of the music.

There are times when both English and Spanish versions of a song exist. Although they are very nice, the English lyrics are usually nothing like the Spanish original, so I encourage you to find an English translation to the song instead of listening to the English version.

I can't imagine a world without music. Can you?

Papi Before and Now

Understand that Papi was not the favorite parent. Far from it. Most of my life I thought of my mother as a saint, and my father as a devil. I knew him mostly as impatient, selfish, and angry. He didn't believe in God or himself. And he physically lashed out at my mother and my siblings.

I wish I could forget what I've forgiven.

Late in life, in his 70s, Papi was reborn by the love of Christ. Peace, joy, understanding and empathy replaced impatience, selfishness and anger.

He was diagnosed with Alzheimer's in his early 80s. Now, in his 90s, the disease has advanced, further transforming him.

He is happy. He smiles, he laughs, and he sings! A carefree little child that brings joy wherever he goes. Now he is my *little boy*.

He is my **good** *little boy*.

Hurricane Maria

There is a story I'd like to tell before I write about Papi (my daddy).

On September 20, 2017, Hurricane Maria devastated Puerto Rico. Papi had been living at a truly wonderful assisted living facility in Gurabo. My brother, Joey, lives in Las Piedras and was called the day prior to come and get Papi. They were evacuating the facility due to the close proximity of the town's river. There was a curve in the river where the facility, Dad's home, was located. Good thing they did.

Months later I visited Puerto Rico and saw what was left of the facility; it had been a two-story high building and housed probably 100 people. The second story was completely gone!

The room that had belonged to Papi was completely gone!

Ten days after Hurricane Maria ravaged Puerto Rico I finally heard from my sister-in-law, Rae, as she stood on the side of a small section of highway in Caguas to get cell service. People lined up in their cars, or on foot, in order to reach their loved ones. She told me that Papi was running out of his medications! My brother was on a mission to find a doctor that would prescribe Papi's Alzheimer's medications; the local hospital had been *destroyed* and Papi's doctors could not be found.

After finding a doctor and obtaining prescriptions, my brother's next mission was to actually *find* the medications. Limited pharmacies. Limited meds in pharmacies.

Pray!

Rae said Joey had two pleas for me: "Get us out of Puerto Rico and find a home for Papi!"

A Lonely Widow

Three years earlier, in the fall of 2014, my Yorkie Abby and I had been on our usual walk through our neighborhood. A neighbor stopped me to ask if I could befriend a lonely widow who was originally from Spain. They had tried helping her but she knew no English; since I know Spanish, they asked if I could help. I thanked them for the information, then sat on that knowledge for a couple of weeks. I had such a "busy" schedule, with working full time … in my mind, there were all sorts of reasons why I had no time for her.

Then I read in the Holy Bible — in James 1:27 — that true religion is taking care of the widows and orphans. I thought, *Who else will help her? Who else in our neighborhood can speak fluent Spanish?*

This was bigger than me, and that's when I knew it would be me.

I began to visit Tina with Abby. I'd take Tina out to dinner. Take her shopping. She was such a joy to be with. A tiny, sweet lady. She stole my heart. I couldn't wait to do things with her. She would ask, "Why do you visit me? Why do you spend time with me?"

I'd say, "Because you're worth it. Now we are family." And, indeed she was.

I'd take Tina grocery shopping, but her idea of food was chocolates and beer. Ay, ay, ay. I'd ask, "Don't you want some milk, orange juice and eggs, too, Tina?" She would grudgingly buy them, but I knew she was only interested in the chocolates and beer.

I knew Tina should not be living by herself. She really needed someone to care for her. Sure enough, one day in the summer of 2015, her neighbor found her lying unconscious in the street. She was rushed to the ER suffering from malnutrition. I visited her in the hospital and in rehab. Her sons found an assisted living home for her where the owner and his wife spoke fluent Spanish.

I visited Tina at her new elderly home, and took her out to dinner and to the local shops. They were such fun outings for us. She loved it when I came. The owners of the home loved it when I visited because Tina came to life. I continued to do this for the next few years.

The Desperate Search

After hearing from Rae I desperately began searching for a home for Papi. Charlotte was way too expensive, so I looked as far as Rock Hill and Catawba, both in South Carolina. I found a wonderful place that didn't appear beautiful on the outside, but the moment I walked in I felt the warmth and love that permeated it. Residents walking up to the owner and calling her "Mom." Residents laughing and smiling. There were eight acres of country that reminded me of Puerto Rico and I knew it would be perfect for Papi. He would love it.

Except ... Papi was a fall risk, and there were stairs. Even the nice porches had stairs. It was culturally diverse, with blacks and whites, but no Hispanics. No Hispanic residents or staff. None who spoke Spanish. I'd already seen how important that had been for Tina.

I found another state-of-the art facility. It was gorgeous. Chandeliers in the wide foyer. Beautiful furniture and rooms. But I felt no warmth. It felt sterile. Residents sat watching television while staff gathered separately, spending time with each other but not with the residents. I longed to find a place that would treat Papi with worth. He may have had Alzheimer's, but he was still alive!

I asked the salesperson if they had staff that spoke fluent Spanish, explaining that as Papi's Alzheimer's progressed, he regressed to his original language, Spanish. She said, "No, but we once had a Hispanic resident and had gotten to the point where we could phonetically figure out a handful of Spanish words he said. We wrote these, and their English translations, on a 2 x 4 card so the staff would know what he was saying."

I burst into tears. How could I have Papi live in a home where he could not be understood? This was more than I could bear.

I thanked her for her time and left.

It was Thursday, October 12. My brother, sister-in-law, and Papi were due to arrive the following Tuesday, October 17. I had no peace regarding a home for Papi. The last thing my father needed was to be living in a place where he couldn't communicate. How confusing that would be to him with his Alzheimer's, especially after living in Puerto Rico.

I pleaded with God: "God, thank You for the miracle of not letting Papi perish with Hurricane Maria. Please help me find a home where he will get the care he needs, a home with heart, and that speaks Spanish."

I totally left the problem with God and that night I had a fitful sleep.

The following morning, when I awoke, I could not get the home where Tina lived out of my mind. They spoke Spanish. Fluent Spanish. But I argued with God: "How can I consider Tina's home when there is only room for six residents and the home is full?" The last time I was there everyone had been very much alive. Still, I could not get the home out of my mind.

I finally called and spoke with Manuel, the owner and main caretaker. I explained to him the situation. How Hurricane Maria destroyed my father's home. How he had advanced Alzheimer's and I could not properly care for him. How he was arriving in five days and I didn't have a home for him. Could he recommend a home for my father?

Manuel simply replied, "We just lost someone, and if your father needs a home, he has a home here."

Just like that. Without meeting my father. Just by knowing me from my visits with Tina. This was a **_huge God moment_** for me.

God knew years ago that Hurricane Maria would devastate my father's home in Puerto Rico.

God knew years ago that my father would need a new home in North Carolina.

God knew years ago that He would bring that person from Tina's elderly home to heaven, just when my father needed a home.

God knew Tina needed a caring friend.

What if I'd never befriended Tina? What if I'd used the excuse of being too busy?

Where would that have left Papi?

"True religion is to care for the *widows* and the orphans." God's words in James 1:27.

In His great care and love for my father, God had worked out all the details.

All I'd had to do was care for, and love, Tina.

Stepping Into Papi's World

The best advice I ever received in dealing with Papi's Alzheimer's came from Carol Howell in her book *Let's Talk Dementia*. It is this: Papi will not and cannot enter into my world; I must enter into *his* world.

I give up my expectations that Papi could ever regain his memories or be able to make new memories. The area that stores memories in his brain has physically deteriorated and there is no way to retrieve them. All Papi can do is live in the moment.

So why fight it? I join him. I step into Papi's world.

There is no agenda. I leave the cares of this world behind. I learn to relax and live in the moment with him.

I find this to be a wonderful revelation: Being with Papi, instead of being stressful, is a very relaxing time for me.

10/24/17 Bésame Mucho

It is my second visit to see Papi in his elderly home. He is sitting in the living room with the other five residents. Five women. He is the only male there, other than Manuel the caretaker. Manuel knows Papi likes to sing, so he loads a CD of Andrea Bocelli and queues it to "Bésame Mucho." We listen to Andrea's beautiful voice, and Papi joins him for a beautifully sung duet. Papi sings strong and loud. He sings on pitch. He leans forward in his seat, really engaged, and really enjoying himself. I observe. I enjoy seeing him and hearing him sing. The song comes to a crescendo and then ends. All the women in the room clap. Papi beams with pride. Are they clapping for him? Are they clapping for Andrea? It doesn't matter. Papi receives the audience's response whole-heartedly.

This song was written in 1940 by a 16-year-old Mexican girl, Consuelo Velazquez. Her circumstances aren't known; maybe she had never been kissed. Maybe she was going to be married soon, as young weddings were customary. Maybe her parents did not approve of him or they were moving away. With World War II underway in Europe and the world in a state of unrest, maybe she feared tomorrow was not promised to their love. A very romantic song for such a young person.

11/04/17 BENDICIÓN

In Puerto Rico it is customary to ask the blessing from an elder in the family. I grew up in New York City *without* this custom. My dad was an atheist most of his life. Late in life he came to believe in God, and Jesus as savior. Now for the first time in my life, Alzheimer's and all, I ask my father for his blessing.

"Bendición, Papi." (Bless me, Daddy.)

"Dios te bendiga, mi hija." (God bless you, my daughter.)

He doesn't hesitate to give me his blessing. He also calls me his daughter. **A double blessing!**

12/01/17 DIOS ESTÁ CONMÍGO

Manuel shares that Papi teaches him what simple faith in God is. He tells me that at night, when he puts Papi to bed, he says to Papi, "Que duermas bien." (Have a good sleep.)

Papi responds, "Yo siempre duermo bien porque Dios está conmígo." (I always sleep well because God is with me.)

This is the man who *didn't* believe God existed most of his life. I'm reminded of the words of Jesus: "Truly I tell you, anyone who will not receive the kingdom of God *like a little child* will never enter it." (Mark 10:15 NIV)

12/06/17 Saying Goodbye for Today

After my time with Dad I say goodbye.

"Es tarde. No quiero que me coja la noche. Me voy pero vuelvo. Te quiero mucho Papi." (It's late. I don't want to drive in the dark. I'm going, but I'll return. I love you very much, Papi.)

"Y yo te quiero mucho también, mi hija." (And I love you very much too, my daughter.)

It's not getting dark yet, but he doesn't know that. I say this because it makes the *moment of parting* easier for him; he wouldn't want me to drive in the dark. I also give him my promise that I'll return, so that *at this moment* he has something to look forward to.

Through my life we had never said the "I love you" words. This has been one of the greatest gifts Papi's Alzheimer's has given me.

December 2017 Christmas

This is Papi's first Christmas at his new home.
Manuel sends me plenty of pictures.

12/08/17

All the residents are wearing Santa Claus masks. With red hats and full cotton beards. They all look so funny. Manuel wears a mask and gets in on the fun with them.

Having fun at Christmas. Papi is standing.

12/09/17

Papi is sitting across from the Christmas tree. His eyes are shining as bright as the Christmas lights. Papi's face glows with a smile. Christmas is indeed for children.

12/23/17

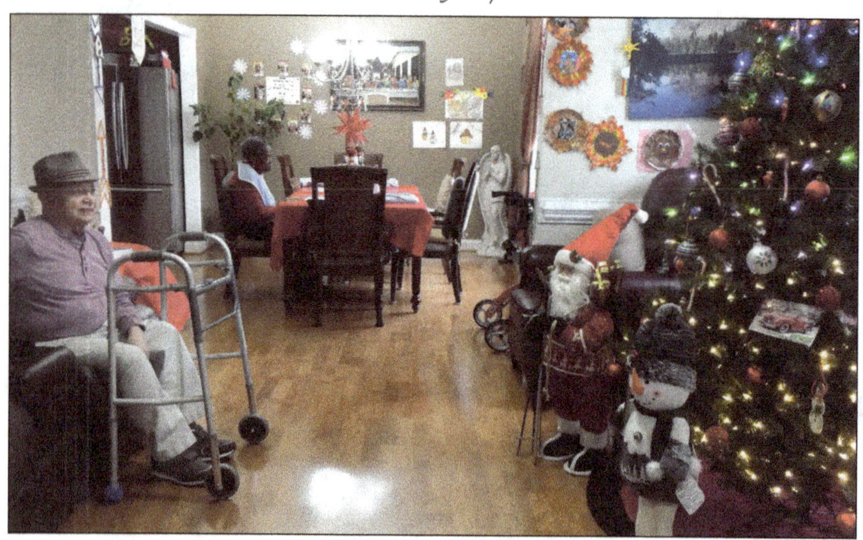

Papi gazing at the Christmas tree.

My husband Tommy and I perform Christmas music for Papi and the folks at his elderly home.

Christmas with a Latin flair! Such fun. As we sing the first song Fran and Lilly get up and dance! Tina claps and says, "¡Olé!" Tommy plays a lively flute introduction to "Angels we Have Heard on High"[1] in Salsa style. Toes tap, bodies sway. Papi claps, then declares, "¡Hechale! ¡Yepa! Juega por ahí. ¡Hechale!" (Go for it! Yepa! Play it there. Go for it!) The whole time he is shaking his walker! I'm laughing.

I sing "O Blanca Navidad Sueño" (I'm Dreaming of a White Christmas)[2]. During Tommy's flute solo Fran gets up and dances. Papi, still seated, moves his legs and arms as if doing an exercise routine. He's

---

[1] "Angels we Have Heard on High" originally in French, English lyrics by James Chadwich in 1862.

[2] "White Christmas" by songwriter Irving Berlin.

dancing! These people have rhythm. The song ends. All are laughing and clapping. "Yay! ¡Muy Bien!"

I sing "Alma con Alma"[3] (Soul to Soul), thinking that Papi would

Fran and Lilly get up and dance.

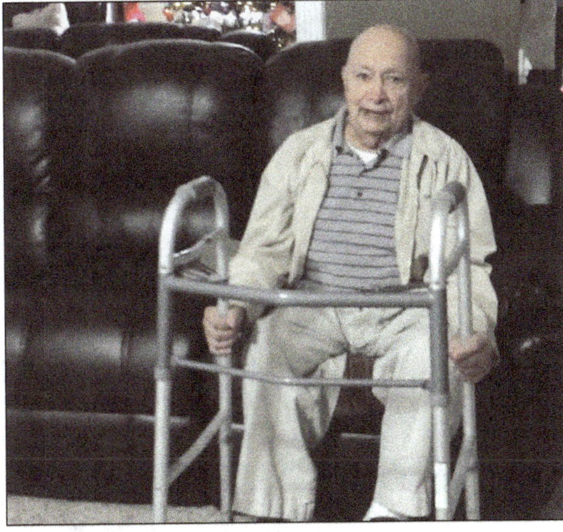

Papi shaking his walker. ¡Hechale!

recognize this old classic.

He springs out of his chair and walks over to me, without his walker, ready to sing. As it turns out *I* sing, and he *tries* to sing. Saying or singing a word or two here and there. He doesn't carry the tune. He doesn't recognize it. He doesn't give up. He improvises. I crescendo at the end of the song and end with "Eh!" which he repeats "Eh!" We laugh and hug.

[3] "Alma con Alma" by Cuban songwriter Juanito Márquez.

Singing "Son de la Loma."

Next song I sing is "Son de la Loma"[4] (Song of the Hill). A song I know he knows. He knows it so well he sings a little ahead of the music. He sings the tune in perfect pitch. Sings with gusto. Tommy ends with a flute solo. Fran dances. ¡Olé!

I sing "Moon River."[5] Lilly sings a duet with me. She has a beautifully clear, pure, soprano voice. As I dip into low notes she goes up an octave. On pitch. A beautiful sound.

Fran slowly gets up and dances. Moving her arms. "Moon River, *wider* than a mile;" Fran spreads her arms out. "You heart breaker;" Fran puts her hands over her heart.

She moves with grace and finesse. A beautiful sight. Papi sings a note here and there.

The song ends with Tommy's flute. Tina cheers Tommy's flute-playing: "Bravo! ¡Fantastico!"

We end our time with "The Christmas Song."[6] I sing "Chestnuts roasting on an open fire … Merry Christmas to you! Merry Christmas to you!" as I point to each of them.

Papi sings, "Meri Krihmas to joo."

I change some lyrics, "…to kids from one to 102." After all, some are over 92!

---

4   "Son de la Loma" by Cuban songwriter Miguel Matamoros.
5   "Moon River" by songwriters Johnny Mercer and Henry Mancini.
6   "The Christmas Song" by songwriters Robert Wells and Melvin H Torme.

Fran dances. "Reindeer really know how to fly…" Fran's arms spread up and across the air.

Tommy's flute-playing shines. Tina stays seated, but Manuel holds Tina's hand and they move their arms together, as if dancing.

I point to each of them as I sing, "Merry Christmas! Merry Christmas! Merry Christmas to you!" We end with clapping, laughing and many happy exclamations.

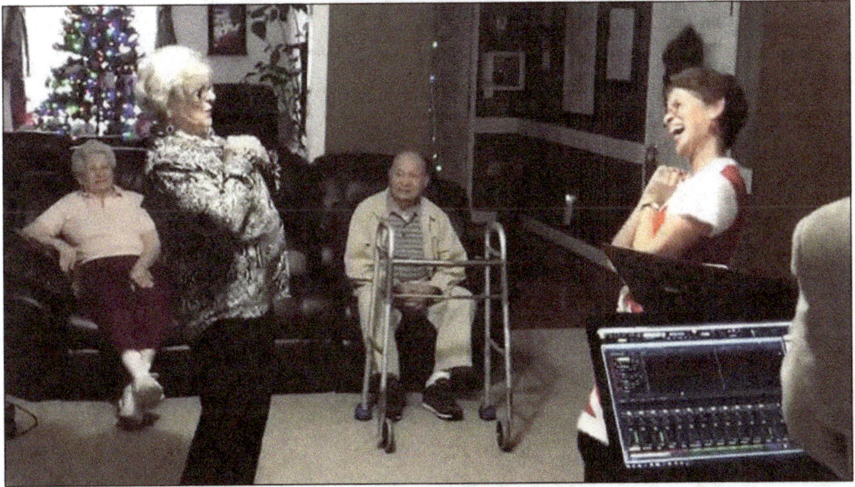

Top: *Wider* **than a mile! … Bottom: You heart-breaker!**

Above,
very merry
Christmas
celebration!

Left, Papi
points to the
colors on the
Rubik's Cube.

Tina gets up and goes over to Tommy, "¡Excellente! ¡Bravo! ¡Esa flauta es magnifica!" (That flute is magnificent!)

I give Papi Christmas gifts I brought for him. I'd gotten him a Rubik's Cube because of the colors. I sit and teach him how he can move the cube around to change the colors.

He points to the colors and says, "Rojo, azul, verde, amarillo." (Red, blue, green, yellow.)

12/25/17

Papi is seated, wearing a new winter hat and a collection of flannel shirts hanging off his arms. Manuel bought him these gifts.

Over the next few years I hardly have to buy Papi clothes. Manuel says it's not necessary for me to do so, as he will do it. He knows every aspect of Papi so well. Manuel shops and buys clothing for Papi, even shoes.

Papi with his Christmas gifts from Manuel.

Living in Papi's World

Every day Papi gcts some exercise; after breakfast and after lunch. Sometimes he walks, sometimes uses the stationary bicycle, sometimes he exercises in place. Today I arrive at Papi's home in time to see him walk indoors with his walker. He goes in a circle from the living room to the front room, to the dining room (where he stops to look out the window), to the kitchen, to the breakfast nook and back to the living room. Then he goes down the hallway leading to the

Papi looks out the dining room window.

bedrooms, back and forth a couple of times. Finally, he approaches the living room sectional sofa and plops down at the far-left end, propping his walker in front of him.

He has learned that this is his designated spot. The residents each have

**Top, Papi goes for an indoor walk.
Above, Papi shares his banana.**

their designated sitting places in a semi-circle in the living room.

Then it is time for his mid-afternoon snack. He always gets something healthy, like fresh fruit. Nothing out of a can or processed. He's given a banana. He's adept at peeling it.

He looks at me and asks, "¿Quieres?" He wants to share his banana. How sweet.

"Sí, Papi."

So he breaks the banana and hands me half. We are sitting on the living room sofa enjoying our banana together. He relishes it, smacking his lips. I relish *the moment with him, and* the banana.

Papi is wearing his favorite hat. Even indoors. Puerto Rican men are taught to remove their hats indoors. That's proper etiquette. But Papi loves this hat, the beige tweed Panama hat he wore when he came from Puerto Rico.

01/09/18 Walk Around the House

It's winter. Papi is not wearing his Panama hat, but instead wears the knitted hat Manuel bought him for Christmas. When Papi retired, he moved back to Puerto Rico; I'm not used to seeing him wearing winter clothing or winter hats. The cold doesn't stop Manuel from bundling everyone up. They go for a walk outdoors, just around the house. Out the front door, around the side, up a ramp to the back porch and back inside. Papi is leading the way. You go Papi!

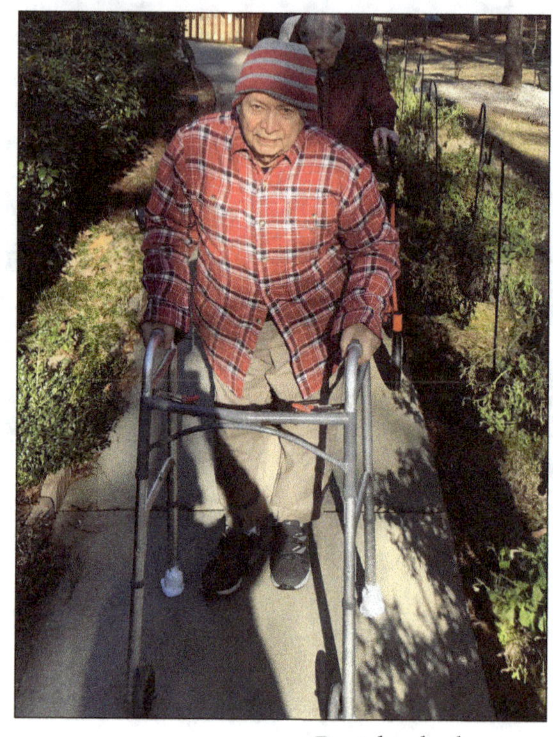

Papi leads the way.

01/11/18 Frisbee

Today the residents of the elderly home are playing Frisbee indoors. They sit in a semi-circle in the living room. Manuel gives each one a soft Frisbee and then he holds up a soft target. Papi inspects the Frisbee, handling it, turning it this way and that. Manuel tells Papi to hit the target with the Frisbee. Papi is not sure what to do. So Manuel asks Lilly to hit the target with her Frisbee and she does. Manuel asks Papi again. Papi is holding the Frisbee in his left hand (my left-handed Daddy) and swings the Frisbee back and forth, back and forth. He continues to do this for a while. Lilly says, "Throw it already!" Papi lets it go and it falls to the floor.

Manuel exclaims, "Wow, that was close! Try again." He hands the

Frisbee back to Papi. Papi sits up in his seat. Leans forward, stretches his left arm out with the Frisbee in his hand. Taking aim, he swings the Frisbee back and forth a couple of times. Then he releases the Frisbee. It flies about eight feet and hits the mark!

Manuel exclaims, "Wow, you did it!"

I shout, "¡Muy bien, Papi!" Papi smiles.

Papi takes aim ... Throws the Frisbee ... *And hits the mark!*

HUMACAO

Papi has told Manuel where he comes from many times. "Soy José Ramón Peña Hernández de Humacao."

Sometimes when Manuel wants Papi to get up and move he says to Papi, "Don Joe, vamos para Humacao."

Papi gets right up and follows Manuel. It doesn't matter that they never actually get to Humacao, the *trip* makes Papi feel like he has gone somewhere.

Sometimes it's only to the bathroom, to pee or poop!

01/11/18 SIEMPRE ALEGRE

Papi loves to sing. I love to hear him sing. Today I sit next to him in the living room and ask him to sing. He sings "Siempre Alegre" (Always Happy).[7] He sings the chorus over and over. Never the verses.

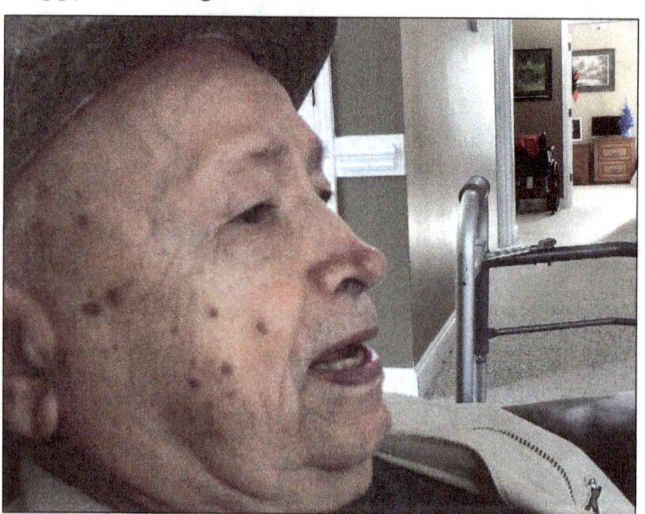

Papi sings Siempre Alegre. *Le lo lai, Le lo lai.*

The chorus is about always living life happily and enjoying all good things because life is short. There are many "Le lo lais" in it. *Le lo lai* is heard in many Puerto Rican songs. It is *the* Puerto Rican melody of happiness.

I sit and take it all in. He completely gives himself to the song. Such happiness! I love it!

---

7   "Siempre Alegre" by Puerto Rican songwriter Manuel Jimenez.

01/18/18 Birdsong

I sit with Papi in his room. The bird feeders outside his panoramic window are full, and birds are coming to feast. Papi and I sit watching the birds, describing their size and colors. He especially likes "el Colorado," the red one. Cardinals come often.

I suddenly hear Papi whistling. He is mimicking the birdsong. In perfect notes. Many birds start to flutter outside his window! Papi says, "¡Mira, mira! Le gusta cuando uno le canta." (Look, look! They like when someone sings to them.)

I'm transported…

I'm a child of eight or nine years old. We walk as a family, my parents and siblings together, to the local park. It is quite a number of city blocks away. Maybe even 20 blocks. Crotona Park. It is the only place in New York City that I personally know where there are trees,

Top, the bird feeder outside Papi's window. Above, Papi enjoying the birds at the birdfeeder.

green grass, flowers, benches, swings, squirrels, and birds.

Later in life I come to call my backyard in North Carolina "My Private Park," as there I have trees, green grass, flowers, benches, swings, squirrels, and birds.

Papi is on the way to see "el juego," the game: baseball played by local

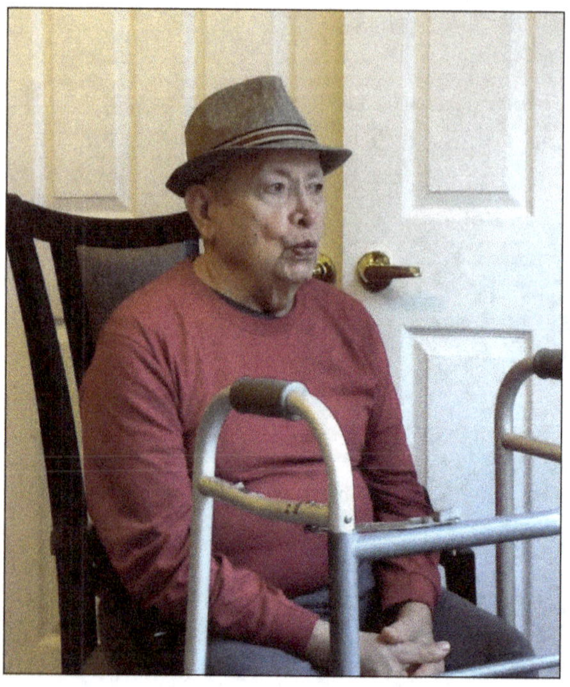

Papi mimics the birdsongs.

Hispanics, mostly Puerto Ricans. On the way I chase squirrels; they're so cute! Also on the way, my father starts to whistle, mimicking the birdsongs. He sounds happy. I can't whistle. I'm fascinated by his ability and enjoy listening to him. As he looks at me, I know he sees this, and this adds to his happy whistling. One of the rare times I see joy in him. We have connected. My Papi loves me.

01/19/18 DR. SNAIDECKI

Papi has an appointment with his geriatric doctor, Dr. Snaidecki. Manuel's wife, Sharon, drives Papi. I meet them halfway. Papi is grinning when he arrives. He is happy to be on an "outing." He's all smiles in the waiting room.

We go in with the nurse and I say to Papi in Spanish, "She wants to hear you sing." He promptly begins to sing "Son de la Loma" as she takes his vitals. Blood pressure, pulse, oxygen, lungs … all his vitals are good.

The doctor comes in. He's not Hispanic but asks Papi, "¿Cómo estás?" Papi responds, "Bien."

Then I say to Papi in Spanish, "He wants to hear you sing."

So Papi laughs and sings "Son de la Loma." Everyone smiles. They don't know what he's singing, but they can see that Papi is happy.

02/03/18 Playing Guitar and Christmas Memories

Prima-hermana (cousin-sister; she's like the older sister I never had) Maria has shared the CD collection *Cien Canciones Puertorriquenas del Milenio* with me, to share with Papi. One Hundred Puerto Rican songs of the Century. That century was the 1900s. Papi's century.

I visit Papi in his room. I put a CD in the CD player the home has provided for him. The music starts with Puerto Rican style guitar picking. I see Papi's left hand start moving, up and down near the area of his belly. Ever so slightly, but evenly, to the music. He is playing a guitar!

His eyes are closed as he strums. At times he moves his fingers independently. Picking the guitar strings! I'm still observing. He is totally immersed in the experience.

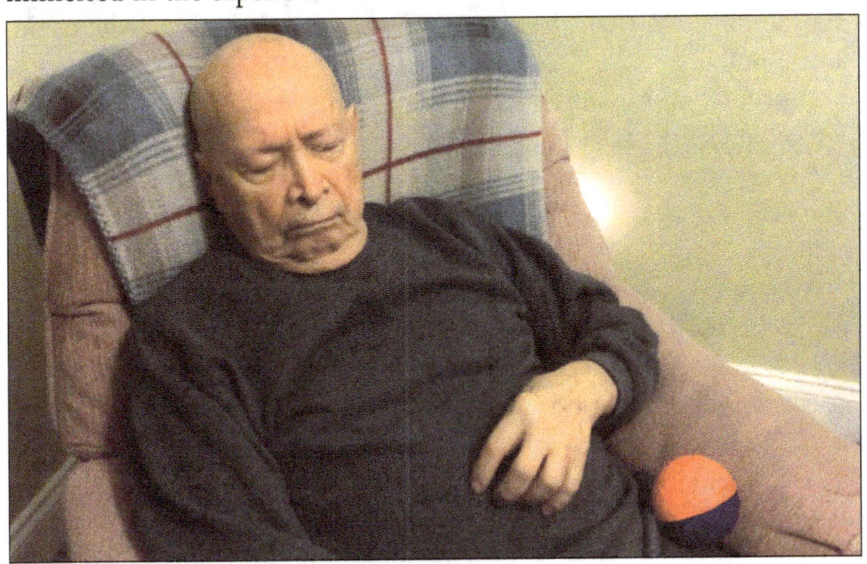

Papi picking the "guitar strings."

I am transported…

I remember a time when I must have been four or five years old. We lived in New York City and there was a snowstorm. It was Christmastime and my family was visiting friends and relatives.

We stand in a Bronx tenement hallway, outside someone's apartment door, singing Spanish Christmas carols. My father and a younger gentleman both have their acoustic guitars. While Papi and the younger man play their guitars, others accompany with maracas and el guido.

The door opens to smiles of welcome. "Entren." (Come in.) We go in and have some refreshments. Drinks for adults and hot chocolate for the children. This scene is repeated a few times during the evening: a Parranda! The Puerto Rican equivalent to Christmas Caroling, but instead of warm, tropical weather we drive from tenement building to tenement building, through a blizzard! We finally settle in an apartment where the music continues till 4 a.m. with Papi and the young man playing their guitars.

The Parrandas didn't continue. A few years later, when I was maybe 10 or 11, I still loved to sit near my father as he quietly sat and played his guitar. He was left-handed, so it had strings that were strung in the opposite direction than the norm, which meant nobody but he could play his guitar.

I recently discussed Papi's guitar playing with my older brother Joey. He tells me that when we were very young our father and uncle — Papi's youngest brother, Robertito — formed a band and would play for special occasions. They especially liked playing for the Parrandas at Christmastime.

My brother recounts how Papi and he would spend time with Robertito and his sons. Joey's cousins were his playmates. It was their guy time, so needed by my brother since he had three sisters and no brothers.

Robertito contracted Bilharzia, a parasitic worm, in a river in Puerto Rico and moved to New York City for medical treatments. The treatments were so painful he started skipping them. It eventually cost him his life. His widow went back to live with her parents, and my brother never saw his cousins again. A great loss for Joey. A great loss for Papi. It ended Papi's guitar playing in a band. His beloved little brother Robertito was gone, taking Papi's joy of playing guitar with him.

My aunt Carmencita, Papi's little sister, told me the widow had been pregnant at the time of her husband Robertito's death. She had twin girls, but Titi Carmen never knew them.

A great loss for our entire family.

02/19/18 Papi at the Fountain

A beautiful three-tiered water fountain sits in front of Papi's elderly home, surrounded by six comfortable lawn chairs for the residents. Papi is sitting there with the others. He stands up and walks to the fountain *without* his walker. He puts his fingers in the water to feel it. He notices something bright at the bottom of the fountain. He rolls up his sleeve and puts his hand in the water. He reaches for the bright thing and lifts it out of the water. He inspects it and says, "Brillante." (Bright.)

Papi at the fountain.

Manuel says to him, "Ponlo en la agua, Don Joe." (Put it in the water, Don Joe.) And he does what he is told, smiling. He always does what he is told, smiling, laughing.

My father is my good little boy. He is also a ***curious little boy.***

Look what I've done!

Each resident gets a fruit popsicle. The popsicle has two sticks. Papi eats half so that one stick separates from the other half. He ends up with a stick in each hand. Happy with what he has accomplished, he holds both hands up in the air to show them off.

Papi does not have his hat on. The hair on the sides of his head is gone! Shaved. Although he had lost the hair at the top of his head, he'd still had hair. It takes me some time to get used to seeing Papi with no hair. But he's usually wearing his hat, so it really doesn't matter.

He lifts both arms up and I think he's going to do some arm stretches, but instead he runs his fingers along the *bald* sides of his head as if running them through his hair. He does this a few times. Then he "pats his hair in place" and brings his arms down!

I guess Papi is not used to being bald either.

Papi has a new pair of shoes on. While seated he reaches down and feels the shoes. I can't get over his flexibility. He knocks on the front tip of the left shoe. Tap, tap, tap. Then says, "Vamos a ver si aprendo hacer algo aquí." (Let's see if I can learn something here.) Then he proceeds to remove his left shoe with the tip of his right shoe. Pop! It's off. LOL!

Papi inspecting his new shoes.

02/28/18 Quizás and Banana

Today Papi is seated around the fountain with the other residents and Manuel. He has a banana in his hand which he peels, then bites into, chews and swallows.

"Dulce," he says. (Sweet.)

Manuel says, "Cántanos una canción, José." (Sing us a song, José.)

Papi laughs and points at the fountain saying, "Ahí. Ese está cántando." (There. That one is singing.)

Manuel asks: "¿La fuente? (The fountain?)

Papi responds: "Sí. La Fuente."

Then Papi holds the banana up and declares out loud (while chewing), "Hay que vivir alegre, y gozar, y olvidarse de las penas." (You must live happy, and have fun, and forget all sadness.)

Such sage advice from my little boy.

Manuel again says, "Cántanos una canción, José."

Papi sings "Quizás."[8] (Perhaps.) A Spanish classic that is world famous. He sings it so well. The melody, perfect.

But sometimes he changes the words. He sings, "Cuando, cómo y *cuando*. Tú siempre contes*tando* … quizás." It rhymes! He *makes* it rhyme! It even makes sense. "When, how, when? You're always responding … perhaps." Papi is a *master* of improv! I can't make up lyrics on the fly, but Papi can!

He finishes the song "Quizás, quizás, quizás," emphasizing each word, shaking his banana!

He laughs and asks Manuel, "¿Te recuerda de eso?" (Do you remember it?)

Then he promptly puts the banana in his mouth, chews, swallows and declares "¡Dulcecito!"

Papi sits, looking at the fountain. After a while he says, "¿De dónde empezaría eso? ¿Esa lluvia? ¿El agua?" (From where does that originate? That rain? The water?)

I love listening to him.

---

8 "Quizás, Quizás, Quizás" by Cuban songwriter Osvaldo Farrés.

03/06/18 Lab Work

Today I take Papi to Dr. Snaidecki's office for his six-month lab work. While the lab technician takes the blood, I distract Papi. I say, "She wants to hear you sing." I start to sing "Son de la Loma" and he continues to sing the song by himself. The distraction works. The blood is taken and it's over before he is done singing.

03/31/18 Bubble Wrap

Manuel comes up with great ideas for the residents to have something new to do. Today it's popping bubble wrap! Each gets a section of it to pop. It works.

They diligently pop the bubbles. Papi completely gives himself to the task, fully satisfied with doing a great job.

Pop, pop, pop!

04/05/18 Lazy 5 Ranch

Manuel takes the residents to Lazy 5 Ranch for an outing. Today Papi sees llamas and pigs, all sorts of animals as they drive through the ranch. Even buffalo! Manuel sends me pictures after the outing, including some pictures of the animals.

But the picture I like best is of the group in the van. Papi has a toothy smile. He is *really* liking it. I know that the van ride alone would have made him happy. But he is elated at what he sees.

On safari drive at Lazy 5 Ranch.

I am transported… As a child I remember one of my father's few enjoyments was the natural world. Every Sunday evening the family would gather around the television to watch Papi's favorite show: *Mutual of Omaha's Wild Kingdom.* Seeing the animals was something that fascinated him. It instilled a great love for the natural world in me, too.

04/16/18 COUNTING ANIMALS

Today Manuel is doing a brain game with the residents. He takes turns asking each individual for the names of animals. He tailors his request to each person, according to their ability.

He asks one of the Spanish-speaking residents to give him the names of three animals. She seems nervous and belabors the task, coming up with only two answers: "Perro, rata."

From another he asks for the names of five animals. She quickly says, "Dog, rat, cat, horse, chicken, cow, pig, bird, squirrel, rabbit!" rattling off the names of *ten* animals.

Eventually he comes to Papi, of whom he asks for the names of two animals. Papi ponders, swaying back and forth in his seat. Swaying, pondering. Then he says, "Fui a buscar la vaca y volví cargando el cabrito." (I went to get the cow and returned carrying the little goat.)

HA! Both Manuel and I laugh. Manuel tells Papi, "¡Muy bien Don Joe!" Papi smiles.

Now it's my turn to ponder.

He's back in primary school! The teacher has asked him for a sentence with two animals!

It's a wondrous thing to see how Papi's brain works.

I ponder and hold onto this for a long while.

04/26/18 APPLE

Papi crunches down on an apple.

As you may have figured out, I call my daddy, "Daddy." My Papi loves eating apples. He eats one almost every afternoon. He has a system when eating an apple. First he holds the stem with one hand and lets the apple dangle.

Then he spins the apple till the stem comes out. Throwing the stem wherever it falls, he then starts to bite into the apple. *Crunch.* Rapture on his face as he eats.

I ask, "¿Está dulce la manzana?"

He says, "Sí."

04/26/18 Caña Brava

Singing "Caña Brava." … "I don't go further."

Papi sings a lively merengue called "Caña Brava"[9] (Wild Sugarcane). He sings loud and strong.

He gets to the chorus: "Ay, sweet sugarcane, wild sugarcane. Give me a piece, girl, of your sugarcane."

He stops singing and looks at me from the corner of his eye. He says, "Y por ahí. No voy mas." (And on it goes. I don't go further.)

So… he knew the lyrics got a little risqué and stopped! Ha! He's my **good** *little boy.*

---

9 "Caña Brava" is a Merengue by Venezuelan songwriter Antonio Abreu as performed by Dominican singer Johnny Ventura.

04/26/18 Viejo San Juan

I ask Papi to sing another song. He sings "En mi Viejo San Juan"[10] (In My Old San Juan).

He doesn't remember all the words in each verse, but he remembers the entire chorus. The melody is perfect. The song is about someone saying farewell to their homeland of Puerto Rico with the hope of returning again.

When I visit Papi he usually asks where I live, just like he did when I'd visit him in Puerto Rico. So, I tell him I live in North Carolina. He always exclaims how far I've come. Papi does not even know he is not in Puerto Rico; he is in North Carolina, less than an hour away from me.

04/30/18 Happy Birthday

Today Papi turned 92. Oh, his birth certificate says he's 91, but I know better. Back in the old days, fathers of families living in rural areas went to the city to register two or three children at a time. He and his younger sister could *not* have been born three months apart. He is the older one, so he is 92. A mistake was made when they registered this little one!

I visit Papi at his elderly home. I bag my lunch and eat at the table with him and the other residents. Afterwards the birthday cake and birthday hats come out. There are balloons. Papi wears a funny birthday cake hat. He is enjoying it all.

Four of the gals gather around Papi for some pictures. I love what I see. All are engaged. We start to sing the happy birthday song. He sings it too. Even though it's in English he sings along. He doesn't understand that we are singing happy birthday to *him*. When we finish singing, he keeps singing the song. In English *and* in Spanish!

"Happy Birzday to joo, Happy Birzday to joo, Happy Birzday to joo-oo, Happy Birzday to joo.

"Que los cumplas felíz, que los cumplas felíz, que los cumplas felíz, que los cumplas felíz."

Laughing he adds, "¡Bien felíz, felíz, felíz!" (Very happy, happy, happy!)

---

[10] "En mi Viejo San Juan" by Puerto Rican songwriter Noel Estrada Suárez.

Papi turns 92.

Then he sings it in English again. He loves singing it so much, he sings it over and over. Half a dozen times, a dozen times, I lose track. Lilly exclaims, "Enough already!" LOL!

But even that doesn't deter him. He sings his Happy Birzday song at least a half dozen more times before he sinks his teeth into the delectable cake.

05/06/18 CANE CREEK

Manuel takes the residents to Cane Creek Park for an outing! He sends me pictures. A beautiful day, lakeside. They have a picnic sitting on lawn chairs. I know Papi loves this. After lunch one of the park rangers comes along in a golf cart and offers to give each a ride. On his ride Papi laughs and laughs. It is the highlight of the day!

Later in the month I decide to take Papi out to Cane Creek Park. It's only five minutes from his home. Papi uses his walker in the paved handicapped walking lanes. We stop every 20 or 30 feet to rest on a bench. He doesn't seem as nimble on his feet as when he's at his home. Every time we sit, he is not interested in getting up again. But I get him

Picnic at Cane Creek Park.

to get up and keep moving. We arrive by the water and sit.

I point to the ducks in the water.

I point to the man fishing from a boat.

I point to a man fishing with his son on the shore.

I love the sights, but Papi doesn't seem interested.

All of a sudden, there is the sound of a mower across the lake.

Papi points across the lake and says, "Hay algo ahí." (There's something there.)

Then he lifts his arm and points at the sky. Even before I see it, *or hear* it, he hears it. An airplane appears. He follows the airplane across the sky with his finger until it disappears.

We head back to the car. Oops! Papi has had an accident. Number one. I can see it in his pants. I settle him in the car and quickly take him back home, where Manuel promptly takes him to the bathroom to clean and change him. At his home Manuel always keeps Papi immaculate.

Everything is always immaculate. Papi is taken to the potty when he wakes, after every meal, before bed and once in the middle of the night, in order to keep him as clean as possible.

I ponder.

A couple of weeks ago I sat with Papi by the fountain in front of his home. While there he lifted his arm and pointed to the sky. An airplane appeared and he followed it with his finger across the sky till it disappeared. We hadn't had to go to the park for him to enjoy that.

I decide I don't need to take Papi to Cane Creek Park so he can have accidents that overflow his Depends. I can take him *as far as his front yard* and there he will have as rich an experience as he likes!

Keep it simple. Ha!

05/12/18 Siempre Alegre at the Hospital

Today Manuel called to let me know my father has gone limp and is unresponsive. He has called an ambulance but wants to know what hospital to send him to. I ask him to send Papi to the hospital closest to me.

By the time I meet Papi in the ER he is looking alert, so I ask him to sing. He sings "Siempre Alegre" (Always Happy). The staff is amazed. The doctor comes to examine him and asks what's wrong with him. I explain the symptoms he had. Although he appears well, back to his old self, back to baseline, he is admitted to the hospital for further tests and observation. I stay with him. I'll stay day and night as long as he's in the hospital. This is because he is like a big two-year-old that doesn't understand what's going on and needs someone to take care of him.

In the hospital room the nurse removes his Depends without replacing it. I say he is incontinent and needs to wear Depends. She says they do not offer Depends and she gets a portable urinal for Papi. I tell her he doesn't know what it is, or how to use it. She says he has no choice, and he'll have to. At this point the nurse hands the portable urinal to Papi. He takes it and instantly props it on his head like a hat! LOL!

The nurse says the hospital believes it's more sanitary for patients not to wear a diaper! They don't even have Depends in stock! I point out that he makes large messes and they will probably change their minds the first time he goes.

That night at 4 a.m., while Papi is in a deep sleep, I go to the local Walmart and buy a bag of Depends. I don't tell anyone what I've done. Bright and early the next morning the nurse comes to see how Papi is doing. He has done number one, *and two,* in the bed. A *huge* dump! The nurse has to get help. They have to change and bathe Papi, and also have to change *all* the linens on the bed. I bring out a Depends and offer it to them. *They promptly take it and put it on Papi.* From then on Papi never goes without a diaper. The staff uses the ones I brought for him.

Papi is not fazed by any of this. He sings "Siempre Alegre" while on his hospital bed. Sings so strongly I can even see the gold in his teeth!

He is sent for an MRI scan. I go with him. He sings on the stretcher going down the hall. Sings as we wait outside the MRI scanning room. I tell the staff that I don't think Papi will stay still long enough for them to scan. They insist on doing it.

I'm allowed to stay with Papi. I explain to Papi that there will be a loud noise, but only for a little while, and to stay very still. He is willing to cooperate. He is always willing. He's my *good little boy*. They start. He stays still. The seconds tick by. After about 10 or 15 seconds he starts to flail his arms and screams, "¡Ay, ayúdenme! ¡Ayúdenme!" (Ay, help me. Help me!) They abort the scan. Papi comes out of the scary machine.

I hold my child and say to the staff, "No more."

All other tests are inconclusive. The doctor that releases Papi says that for the record they will note he had a TIA, a mini-stroke. I'm so happy that he is back to baseline, and happily singing.

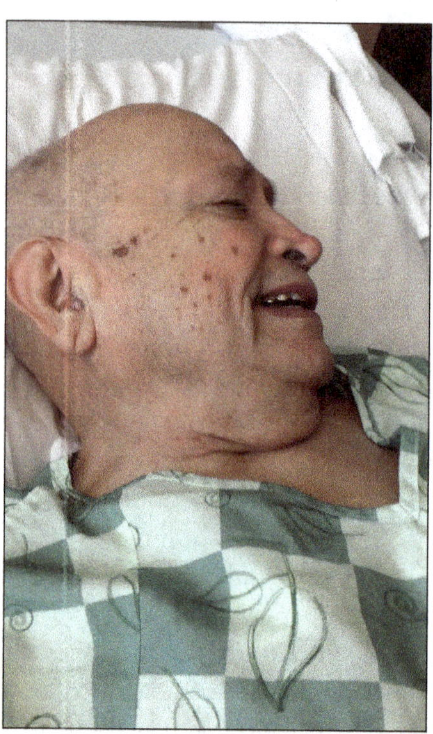

Papi smiles and sings while in the hospital.

A week later I receive a review form from the hospital for *my father to fill out.* I let them know how ridiculous it is *not* to have Depends for Alzheimer's patients and give a detailed account of his *huge dump!*

05/25/18 Hat and Stationary Bicycle

Today I see Papi take his turn on the stationary exercise bicycle. He is alert and his eyes are shining. Papi is keen to do whatever is asked of him. He readily sits on the bicycle. Then Manuel helps put Papi's feet on the pedals.

"Dame cinco minutos, Don Joe." (Give me five minutes, Don Joe.) Papi starts pedaling. When he slows down Manuel says, "Dame cinco minutos mas, Don Joe," and Papi picks up the pace.

He keeps a pretty good pace. This continues for about *20 minutes*, till Manuel says, "Muy bien, Don Joe. ¡Hiciste una milla!" (Very good, Don Joe. You did a mile!)

Papi is happy. He really enjoyed exercising *and* receiving praise for his accomplishment. Very good, Don Joe!

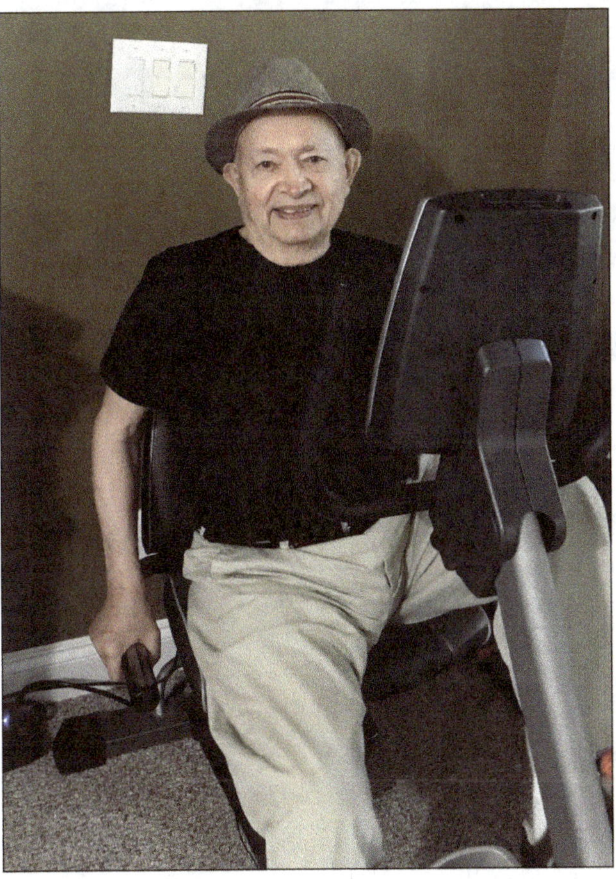

Papi gets his exercise.

06/17/18 A Rich Heritage

I spend time today with Papi in his room. He sits up straight in a chair, wearing his hat and a light jacket. He is in a singing mood and sings two new songs. Actually, they are very old Hispanic songs, but it is the first time I hear him sing them. Two beautiful, sad boleros.

The first is "Inolvidable" (Unforgettable). It is about a lost love that is *unforgettable!* I find it very poignant that as he is *forgetting* his memories, he sings this song. After he sings he says, "Los que uno ama no se olvidan." (You never forget those you love.) I agree. He loves me. I love him. Yet, he does *not* remember Mami (my Mommy), his wife of almost 60 years and the love of his life.

The second song Papi sings is "Llanto de Luna"[11] (Tears of the Moon). In this song a lover laments over a love that is lost by deception, his desire to forget, and the inability to forget. Why are so many love songs sad? Yet, the music is beautiful. I would like my husband to sequence these two songs so that I may sing them to the public. My wonderful husband has already sequenced other songs that Papi sings: "Bésame Mucho," "Quizás," "En mi Viejo San Juan," "Lamento Borincano."[12]

Papi is leaving a rich heritage of Hispanic classic songs through me. My husband sequences, and I sing. The audience in the Charlotte area receives them well. For the non-Spanish-speaking audience I translate some lyrics or share the gist of the song.

The Hispanic audience is diverse. From Puerto Rico, Cuba, Columbia, Costa Rica, Dominican Republic, Peru, Honduras, Mexico, Spain, etc. All clap, all are enthralled.

A young teenager with a heavy Hispanic accent tells me he loves that I sing the classics and he loves my voice.

Others come back with their father or grandfather.

A Hispanic family returns to celebrate a 94-year-old's birthday with four generations of family present.

A young lady cries while I sing "Bésame Mucho" and afterwards says the song was her grandmother's favorite.

Papi, through me, will be touching hearts long after he is gone.

---

[11] "Inolvidable" and "Llanto de Luna" by Cuban songwriter Julio Gutiérrez.

[12] "Lamento Borincano" by Puerto Rican songwriter Rafael Hernández Marín.

06/27/18 ELECTRIC RAZOR

Today I spend time with Papi in his room. Papi sits in his recliner and holds an electric razor firmly in his left hand, slowly moving it up and down the left side of his face. Manuel has patiently taught Papi how to shave himself!

Once in a while, Papi stops to feel the just-shaved-portion of his face to discern whether the shave is close enough or if he needs to shave that area more.

I coach him a little by touching him on the right side of his face saying, "Aquí también." (Here too.)

He puts his right index finger on the spot and asks, "¿Aquí?" (Here?)

"Sí, Papi." He takes the razor up to his finger and slowly shaves that area.

Manuel comes in and shaves the right side of Papi's chin and throat, saying, "Esta area también." (This area too.)

When he goes to shave the left side Papi speaks up: "Dejame tratar," (Let me try,) so Papi slowly shaves the left side of his chin and throat. Papi is still a "can do" kind of person! Each time he shaves he needs to be re-taught, but he enjoys learning so it's okay. More than okay … it's great! Papi then shaves the mustache area under his nose, bringing his upper lip down. Slowly shaves up and down, the entire area.

He feels his face and declares "¡Ya!" (Done!)

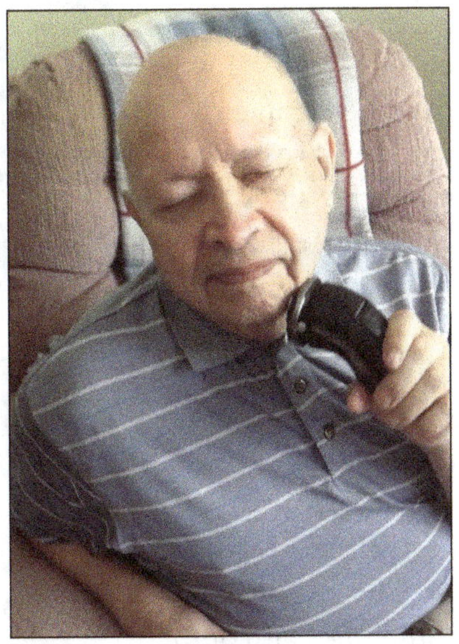

Papi shaves himself.

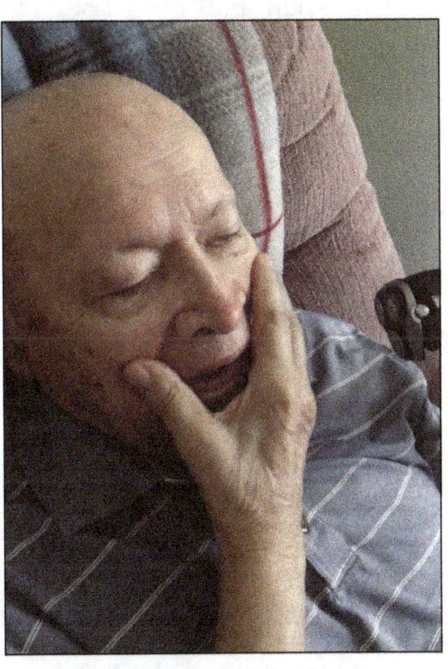

Checking if his face is smooth.

07/04/18 God Bless America

It's the Fourth of July and Papi is watching a patriotic program on the television with the other residents.

He sings the songs. He sings "God Bless America."[13] I love that song.

He sings in English! He rarely *speaks* in English these days, but he can *sing* patriotic songs in English.

Puerto Rico is a commonwealth of the United States.

Papi spent half his life stateside seeking a better economic life for his family.

Papi is *patriotic!* God Bless America!

"God bless America!"

07/10/18 Andrea Bocelli CD

We're in Papi's room. Manuel lends me a CD with Andrea Bocelli singing Hispanic Classics. I put it on and Papi sings a duet with Andrea. "Bésame Mucho." Papi sings with such gusto, emotion and expression. Sometimes closing his eyes, sometimes moving his hands. Sometimes

---

13   "God Bless America" by American composer Irving Berlin.

picking at one of the buttons on his shirt. Ha! The song ends and another begins, but Papi continues to sing "Bésame Mucho." He loves that song.

Then Andrea sings "Somos Novios" and to this Papi sways. He sways to the entire song, with his eyes closed, completely immersed in the music. A smile on his face. Swaying his head, swaying his body, side to side, forward and back. I love watching him.

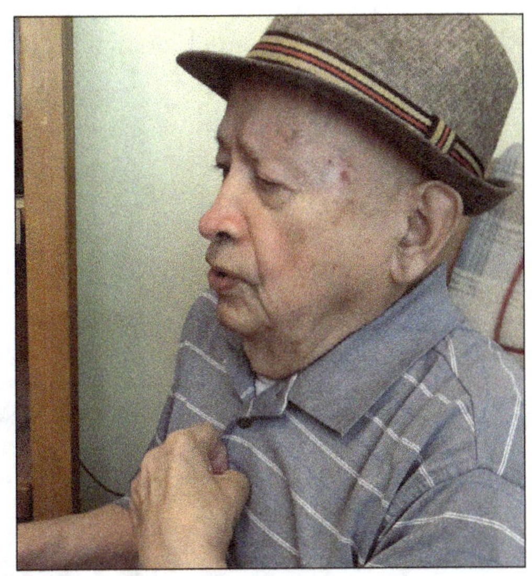

Papi sings, sways and picks at the button on his shirt.

08/17/18 OLD-FASHIONED SHAVE

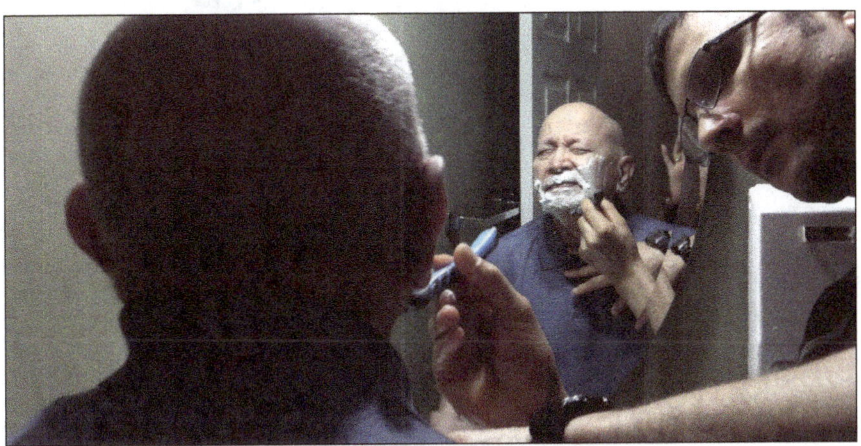

Having an old-fashioned shave.

Today when I arrive at Papi's home Manuel is shaving him the old-fashioned way. Papi is in the bathroom standing before the sink. There is a mirror on the wall and Papi stands before it. I see his face in the mirror. He has shaving cream on his face, eyes closed, standing very still for the shave. Manuel lets Papi know how to move his head. He follows Manuel's instructions very well, shifting his face this way and that. I quietly observe till they are done, then Papi and I go to his room for some time together.

08/25/18 Fountain and Singing

Manuel sends me a video. Papi is seated at the water fountain in front of the house. Papi gets up, takes his hat off. He goes to the fountain, scoops water up in his hand and splashes it on his head! LOL! He must be hot on this August day!

As he sits back down Manuel says, "Cántanos una canción José." (Sing us a song José.)

Tina says, "Sí. Cántanos." (Yes. Sing for us.)

Papi ponders, then sings "Inolvidable" (Unforgettable). He holds his hat upside down, turning it round and round by the rim while he sings. When he finishes the song, he pops the hat on his head and taps it down, punctuating it with a verbal rhythm: "Para-pa-pa, coo coo." He makes me smile!

I'm so glad others appreciate Papi's singing!

Papi cooling off. "Para-pa-pa, coo coo."

09/10/18 Walk Outdoors

I get to Papi's home in time to see them returning from a walk in the neighborhood! I knew they sometimes walked outside, around the house, but here they were coming down the street.

They look so happy.

Manuel pushes one woman in a wheelchair, another holds onto his arm, the rest walk on their own. Tina walks sprightly. Papi uses his walker. Sometimes he bends over too much and Manuel instructs him, "Enderechete, José." (Straighten up, José.) Papi brings himself up.

Manuel tells me they walked to the end of their street and back. There are only a handful of homes on the street and it is lightly trafficked. Manuel says it's a one-quarter mile round trip.

I'm amazed! I didn't think half of them, including Papi, could walk that distance. I'm grateful for what Manuel accomplishes with them. They get fresh air, sunshine and exercise!

Papi's Teeth

09/11/18

Last week Manuel told me that one of Papi's molars had split in two, and he gave me the half that had fallen out of his mouth.

I take Papi to a dentist in Waxhaw, along with his half tooth. They try, but getting x-rays from Papi proves impossible. Papi keeps biting down on the x-ray strips with his front teeth. Then he just sits there and grins.

They tell me the tooth cannot be extracted at the dentist's office. That he would have to be sedated for the tooth extraction and needs an appointment with an oral surgeon. When they try to make the appointment with the oral surgeon, the oral surgeon refuses, due to Papi's Alzheimer's and age.

How frustrating! These two things can't be changed. They are Papi's reality.

How am I supposed to get help for Papi?!

09/13/18

I try a different dentist in Waxhaw. They also are not able to get x-rays. But they are able to take *pictures* showing the broken tooth and some decay on an adjoining tooth. They tell me there is a possibility that *two teeth* would need extraction. They, like the other dentist, say that due to sedation they'd have to make an appointment with an oral surgeon in Monroe.

So, we make an appointment for a consult. Getting closer. At least it isn't flat-out rejection.

09/18/18

Today is the consult at the oral surgeon's office. Large place with lots of staff. First thing they do is take Papi to a small room with a large x-ray machine. He stands before it. The young assistant is sweet and Papi is happy to meet her.

She asks him to put his chin up on the chin rest; he sees himself in the mirror on the wall. He's fascinated by it. "Mira lo que veo ahí." (Look at what I see there.) She tells him to stand still, and he does! He is having a good day, and as usual he wants to please. She quickly steps out and in a few seconds the deed is done. Success. Good x-rays.

They want to make an appointment at the hospital as he will need IV sedation. How complicated! I ask why it can't be done at the office. The oral surgeon asks if he is capable of having an IV. I say he has had a hospital stay with IVs and he is easy to work with. They decide they will do the IV in the office.

We make the appointment for the tooth extractions. They don't take Medicare and it will completely be an out-of-pocket expense. I agree; what else can I do? I will trust that God will continue to provide for Papi's needs.

Papi loves meeting people. On the way out we stop to pay today's bill and I say to Papi, "Look who's here," referring to one of the receptionists. He gives her a big smile. I say, "I think she would like to hear you sing." So Papi sings for her. She stops what she's doing to listen. In a beautiful clear voice Papi sings "Siempre Alegre" (Always Happy).

I translate the song for her.

She says to Papi, "I need to follow that advice. That is wonderful advice. Thank you for sharing that beautiful song with those beautiful words. I will try to follow your example in my life."

The other receptionists behind her all clap.

Papi is all smiles. What joy he brings! What joy he lives! Papi has had a good day. When I take him home he walks down the walkway with Manuel *without* his walker!

Walking with Manuel, without his walker.

10/18/18 ORAL SURGERY

Today is Papi's scheduled oral surgery. He is to have two molars extracted.

He is happy. He never understands where he is going, or why. He is just happy to be going somewhere and meeting new people. This is my dad *now* with advanced Alzheimer's. All my life I had thought of him as mostly antisocial. Wow.

He sits in the surgeon's chair and one of the young assistants says to me she has learned a couple words in Spanish. I tell her to go for it. "Que guapo," she says.

Papi laughs. Then turns to me and says, "Ella cre que soy guapo. Ah, ella cre que soy guapo." (She thinks I'm handsome. Wow, she thinks I'm handsome.)

Sweet!

The anesthesiologist says he spent some years in Peru and starts to speak to Papi in Spanish, with a heavy American-English accent. He lets Papi know he will stick a needle in his arm and Papi says okay. All goes smoothly. As Papi drifts off to sleep, I leave and go to the waiting room.

Half an hour later the surgeon comes to tell me it went well, and that Papi is being wheeled out the back, and for me to drive around and pick him up. Papi is awake but groggy. They help me get him in the car and we drive off. By the time we get back to his home he is totally awake. He hasn't a clue what has transpired. He is his happy self.

It is done! Easy-peasy. Humph! After having been rejected by that first oral surgeon, my father was easy-peasy!

The following spring Papi has another molar split in two. Bottom back. Easy to see. The oral surgeon remembers him and schedules the oral surgery *without* a consult. She knows it will be easy. Papi is easy. They schedule the same anesthesiologist. It goes just as smooth as the last time. I wish I could tell that other oral surgeon that refused Papi! Ha! Ha!

At almost 93 my father's teeth are beginning to fall apart. He's been on Vitamin D and calcium for a while, but still his teeth are disintegrating.

I reminisce.

I remember when I was young. My father, after eating, would chew Dentyne Sugarless Gum or Trident Gum to get food out from around his teeth and keep his mouth fresh. No bad breath. He always carried Dentyne Sugarless Gum or Trident Gum when he was out and about. At home he also used toothpicks to get food out of tighter places. He always had good teeth. Oh well, what can be expected at 92, almost 93?

Life in Papi's Home

10/19/18 Twenty-five Aprils

Papi sings "Tiempos Viejos"[14] (The Old Times) also known as "25 Abriles" (25 Aprils), a bolero. Sings only the chorus. It is a sad man's song, singing to a "brother" about the old times. The 25 young years that will never return. Lamenting to the point of tears.

Then he laughs a little and says, "Ah, se pone triste uno." (Ah, makes one sad.)

He's diffusing the sadness of the song with a little laughter.

I reminisce.

I grew up with the little Spanish children's song "Cielito Lindo"[15] (Lovely Sky). It's one of those "Ay, ay, ay" songs. It's like "Oy Vey," expressing dismay or grief. The advice in this little ditty to children is that instead of crying you can make the heart happy by singing.

It could be Papi's life motto. My simple **song-loving** *little boy*.

10/22/18 Noodles

This morning I visit Papi and it is exercise time. The six residents of the home are seated in a semi-circle in the living room. Each with some level of dementia or Alzheimer's. Some advanced, like my father.

Each is given a pool noodle and a balloon is thrust into the air. Manuel

---

14 "Tiempos Viejos" songwriters M Romero and F Canaro. To find correct version of this song with correct lyrics watch the video by Jose David Soto

15 "Cielito Lindo" by Mexican songwriter Quirino Mendoza Cortés.

calls out to each one to hit the balloon with their noodle as the balloon approaches their area. The idea is to keep the balloon from hitting the floor. They actually get it. Little by little they all come to life. Hitting the balloon. Papi joins. It's something he can do. Maybe it reminds him of his favorite spectator sport, baseball. Ha!

He's loving it. I love seeing him engaged.

11/22/18 Greens and Sweet

I sit near Papi while he's eating lunch at the table. He wears his oversized bib. It covers his shirt and reaches under his plate. Anything he drops will fall on the bib.

Sometimes the food is hot when placed in front of him. So, Manuel warns, "Está caliente, Joe." Papi takes some food on his fork and starts to move the fork around in the

Top, group play. Above, keeping the balloon in the air.

A smile, even eating his greens.

air, like a small airplane. Zoom, to the left. Zoom, to the right. Does this a couple of times before he aims at his mouth and lands the plane! Ha!

Papi sometimes leaves his greens on the plate, after eating everything else first. Then Manuel says, "Cómete lo verde también." (Eat your greens too.) Papi doesn't quibble but picks up his fork and proceeds to eat every bit of his greens. Then with his index finger he "cleans" the plate and puts his finger in his mouth, licking every last bit off.

I wonder, *What was the problem with the greens?*

He takes a swig of juice. I ask him, "¿Eso esta bueno, Papi?" (Is that good, Daddy?)

"¡Si! Esta dulce también." (Yes! It's sweet too.) Then gives me a big smile. Well, he apparently likes sweet foods better. Who doesn't?

11/28/18 Activity Toy

I buy Papi a Fisher Price activity cube. I place it in his hands and watch what he does. One side is orange with three small yellow spinning wheels. He spins the first and it spins freely. He spins the middle one and it creaks, but hardly moves. Then he spins the third and it spins freely. He does it again, then signs to me to pay attention. He demonstrates spinning the three little wheels, then pointing to the middle one he says, "Ese no va." (This one doesn't go.)

Next, he presses the purple buttons on the green side. Then he looks at the yellow side and presses the middle of the long red button in the center. It doesn't move. Instead of pressing the end of the red button he presses all around it, finally pressing the end of the red button, so it goes down.

I ponder whether he was just pretending he didn't know how it worked. I'll never know for sure. He turns the cube to the blue side with the green protrusion. He grabs the green protrusion and tries to turn it, as if to unscrew it, but it does not turn. He puts the cube down.

He is done.

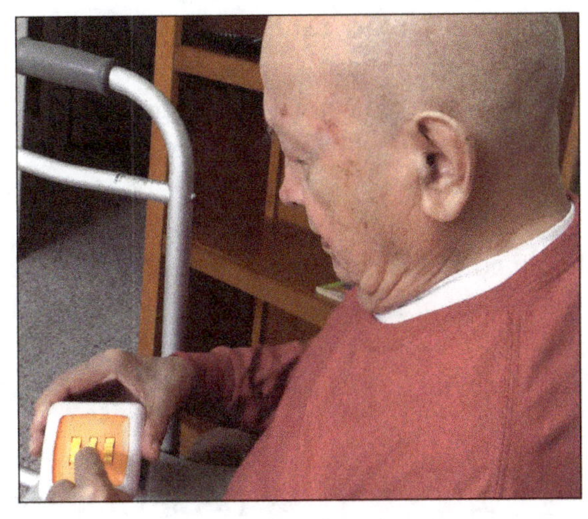

This one doesn't go.

11/28/18 Fidget Spinner

I also buy Papi a fidget spinner. I put it in Papi's hand. I place his index finger on the center of the spinner and his thumb on the other side, and I start spinning it. He's captivated. He says, "Mira. Miralo cómo corre." (Look. Look how it runs.) I say, "Ligerito." (Fast.)

It keeps spinning without slowing down.

He says, "No se cansa. Miralo cómo corre." (It doesn't get tired. Look at it run.)

Pinky in the fidget spinner.

Holding it, he moves his hand up, then down, then in circles all around. It doesn't slow down. He's smiling. He laughs. He brings it with his hand to the other side of his walker. He brings it back. He sticks it below. And brings it up. He touches it lightly and it stops immediately.

I take his other hand and with *his* finger I start it going again. He touches it lightly and it stops. He shows me how he can stick his pinky finger in one of the holes of the spinner.

Then he spins it with his finger, and it runs. He is fascinated. He stops it, then starts it.

This goes on for a while then eventually, while it spins, he sits back holding it till he falls asleep with it in his hand.

I watch him sleep. Eventually I take the fidget spinner from his hand and put it away for another day.

I leave while he's asleep.

11/28/18 BUILDING BLOCKS

Later in the day, after my visit, Manuel sends me pictures. Papi, Tina and Selia are standing around a table. They are working with colored building blocks. Papi lines some side by side on one side of the table, so that they are perfectly aligned, while Tina looks on. When Papi has seven side by side he begins to stack them on the stack in the

Taking turns.

middle, very carefully. One, then two of them. Then Tina takes a turn and stacks one while Papi looks on.

Selia works on her own, lining her blocks up. After a while, Lilly joins them. Papi loves to line the blocks up on his side of the table *before* he takes a turn on the stack. He has 13 lined up. The stack is 15 blocks high! Tina adds to the stack while both Papi and Lilly look on. Papi adds carefully, 18 blocks high! Papi smiles!

They have fun together. They have worked together. Taking turns, like good children.

Steady hands make 18 blocks high.

12/04/18 Exercise Kick and Arms

Today I arrive at Papi's home during their morning exercise. Some routines Manuel leads, some routines are on video. In English. There are three residents that don't understand Spanish. I observe for a while without letting Papi know I'm there. The video demonstrates hands up over head, hands down, then hands up and out to the sides and down. Papi intertwines his hands and raises them over his head, then down, then over his head, then down. No matter what different arm moves are shown on the video, Papi does the same move. It's not perfect, but he's doing it! Exercising his arms.

Then Manuel has them all get up and do squats! He demonstrates and they do the squats along with him. Papi does squats holding onto his walker, but he does it! Then Papi decides to take a walk. I take a seat next to his spot on the sofa. He decides he's going to take a shortcut between Lilly and Fran. Not enough room. Ha! He has to be redirected. He does the circle through the rooms and comes back to sit in his spot on the sofa.

Exercise for mobility.

Papi enjoys showing me what he can do. "Mira." (Look.) Sitting, Papi kicks his right leg up and down, then left leg up and down. Right arm up and down, left arm up and down. He's getting more exercise than I am!

12/04/18 Toys and Dónde Quiera

We sit in Papi's room. I've bought and brought Papi two child beginner toys. I introduce one at a time.

First is a small, stuffed, easy-to-hold dog. Papi smiles and says, "Esta contento" (He's happy) and moves him up and down. Then he sticks the doggy in his belt. LOL! Then I put a ball-within-a-ball rattle in his hands. He shakes it and it jingles. He likes the sound. Sometimes closing his eyes while shaking the ball, listening to it.

Papi with his new toys.

He is getting tired, so I put a CD on. He sits back and starts to sing with the CD, mostly with his eyes closed. Sings "Donde Quiera que Tu Vayas"[16] ("Wherever You Go").

This song expresses the sentiment that even apart, no matter how far, we will be with each other, that love never ends… and will *never be forgotten*.

The song touches me to the core.

12/25/18 CHRISTMAS

It's Christmas again, and Manuel sends me pictures. One shows Papi with his gifts of clothing hanging all over him. He has a new white Panama hat on.

Merry Christmas!

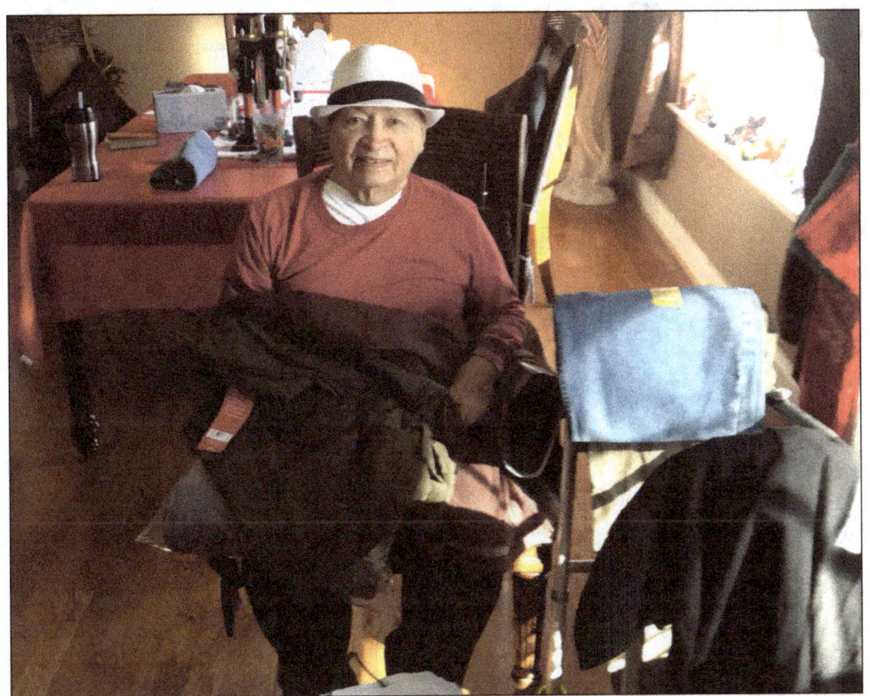

Christmas 2018: Gifts from Manuel.

---

[16] "Donde Quiera que Tu Vayas" by Puerto Rican songwriter Ramón Ortíz del Rivero.

12/27/18 Tommy and Nancy Perform Again

Tommy and I perform again for those at Papi's elderly home. They are engaged but in many of the residents you can see the decline as dementia

Hat off ... hat on.

or Alzheimer's advances. One still sings, another raves over Tommy and his flute-playing, but the dancer teeter totters.

When I sing "Son de la Loma," Papi does not stand up. Last year he stood without a walker. This year he only walks with a walker. He stays sitting but sings along. He is wearing his new white Panama hat, which he apparently likes, as he continually takes it off and puts it back on while he sings. He taps the hat down on his head and fondles the rim. As the songs end, he claps heartily.

At the end of our performance Tina can't contain herself and gets up and walks over to Tommy. "¡Magnifico! ¡Excelente! ¡El mejor flautista que he oído!" (Magnificent! Excellent! The best flutist I've ever heard!) She is expressive as she talks to Tommy and hugs him!

01/04/19 Kick and Count and Maracas

I arrive during their exercise routine. I don't interrupt but I sit and observe. Most sit during the exercise. Papi is sitting. Manuel asks him to do some kicking exercises. He says in Spanish, "Don Joe, give me 10 kicks."

Papi starts kicking and counting, in *English*. Papi actually counts in *English*! He can't converse much in English but he can count. Maybe it's because of the rhythmic pattern.

I hear (and see) Papi: "One (kick), two (kick), three (kick), four (kick), five (*no* kick), six (*no* kick), seven (*no* kick), eight (*no* kick), nine (*no* kick), ten (*no* kick)!"

He's so proud of himself. Only kicked four times, but since he kept counting, he thinks he's done what he was asked to do. Or does he think he's "smart" and believes he tricked us? LOL! Guess we'll never know.

Today before embarking on the 40-minute drive to Papi's home, I had taken a pair of mini-maracas from my dining room curio cabinet. After his exercises, Papi and I go to his room. He moves and walks pretty well with his walker, for which I'm grateful.

Papi deftly plays the maracas.

I stick one of the CDs in the CD player and hit the Play button. Papi listens and sways but doesn't sing. He loves the music. I know he also loves to do something with his hands, so I hand Papi the maracas. He holds them by the handles and clumsily starts to shake them. He says, "Oye." (Listen.) He is fascinated with the sound he's producing with them. Over time he starts to catch the rhythm of a song. Within a few songs he is deftly playing the maracas. Just like a pro. Amazing!

Brings a smile to my face.

01/08/19 DOMINOES

Today when I visit Papi he is playing dominoes. Actually, he doesn't remember how to play dominoes anymore, so he is just putting domino pieces where he is being told they go.

As I was growing up, Papi was the domino champ in our home. He was so good that after a while none of us would play with him. He could beat anyone that would visit us as well. Later in life, at the elderly home in Puerto Rico, he had the honor of being sought out by the other residents as being a great domino player. In his eighties there were many things he couldn't remember, but he was still adept at dominoes.

I remember going to Puerto Rico and spending time with Papi and Mami at the elderly home. They were usually playing dominoes, so I would join them. Mami was never any good at dominoes. I'm not that good at playing dominoes either, although I like to play. I just enjoy the time with others. I'm like my mother in that way; we enjoy being with others.

There was one more person playing with us. We played a handful of games. Papi won every one of them. Then Mami actually won a game. Papi got angry at her and accused her of cheating! After all, *she* never won, *he* did. Mami covered her face to protect herself from the verbal attack.

Papi "playing" dominoes.

I spoke up for her, telling Papi she won fair and square! He still didn't believe it.

I said, "Let's play another game," to try to get him to move on. It took him a while to cool down. He won the next game and all was right with the world. All was normal again. He was the champ!

Most dominoes have only white dots on black, or black dots on white. The dots on the domino set that is used in Papi's home have a different color for every number. This assists the residents with matching the dominoes.

Papi's thinking is much simpler. He can't strategize. He can't even figure out the numbers represented by the dots. He can remember some colors. A few. Rojo (red) is his favorite. Even though he remembers what some colors are called he still doesn't understand how to match the dominoes. He only knows he has a domino in his hand and he has to put it down at the end of the row that's being built. When he puts it down, he feels like he accomplished the point of the game.

"Ahí. Lo puse." (There. I put it.) He feels like a champ.

He is!

UTI, Hospitals and More Fun

06/21/18

Papi is lethargic. A urine sample is taken to Dr. Snaidecki's office. Papi has a Urinary Tract Infection (UTI) and is put on an antibiotic.

07/31/18

Papi is lethargic. A urine sample is taken to Dr. Snaidecki's office. Papi has a UTI and is put on an antibiotic.

08/13/18

Papi is lethargic. A urine sample is taken to Dr. Snaidecki's office. Papi has a UTI and is put on an antibiotic.

01/25/19 – 01/30/19

Papi is lethargic. He is sent to the ER. I meet him there. He has a UTI. He responds well to the antibiotic drip and is himself, singing again, in no time. Yet he is still admitted to the hospital pending further urine tests and results. I sign a Do Not Resuscitate Order. This is a tough thing to do.

This time there are plenty of Depends on hand. Somebody read my review and made changes! Yes! I spend five days, 24/7, in the hospital with Papi. He sings. He laughs. I enjoy being with him and seeing him happy.

02/11/19

I take Papi to a specialist in Monroe, per Dr. Snaidecki's instructions. A urologist that puts Papi on a UTI maintenance drug.

02/20/19

A urine sample is taken to Dr. Snaidecki's office. Finally NO UTI. Hallelujah!

Took eight months to clear!

03/12/19 WHITE HAT AND RED BALL

Today Papi is wearing his white Panama hat. It is one size fits all. It's huge on him! I think it makes him look a little hickish. But that doesn't bother him!

Manuel has attached a red paper-mache ball to the ceiling fan in Papi's room. Manuel did this on Valentine's Day and has left it there because it entertains Papi so much. The bright red color catches Papi's eye. He looks up at it, points and says, "Miralo. Colorado." (Look at it. Red.)

I say, "Sí. Lo es." (Yes. It is.) Rojo and colorado both mean "red" in Spanish.

He continues to stare at it and comment on it: "¡Mira eso!" (Look at that!) Simple joys.

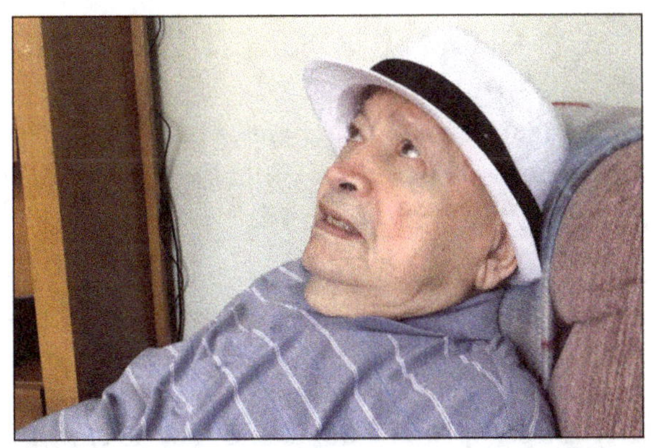

Papi stares up at the paper-mache ball in his room. "Mira eso."

04/06/19 Hospital, No Pain

Today Papi is experiencing fevers, chills and increased confusion. He is sent to the ER. This time he does *not* have a UTI. He is admitted to the hospital. A general antibiotic brings him back to normal, but doctors don't know why he wasn't well.

I'm asked, has he had surgeries? I tell them he'd had his gallbladder removed a few years ago.

We spend five days in the hospital. We sing, and he sings for the hospital staff. I have his beginner toys. He plays with them for hours in his hospital bed.

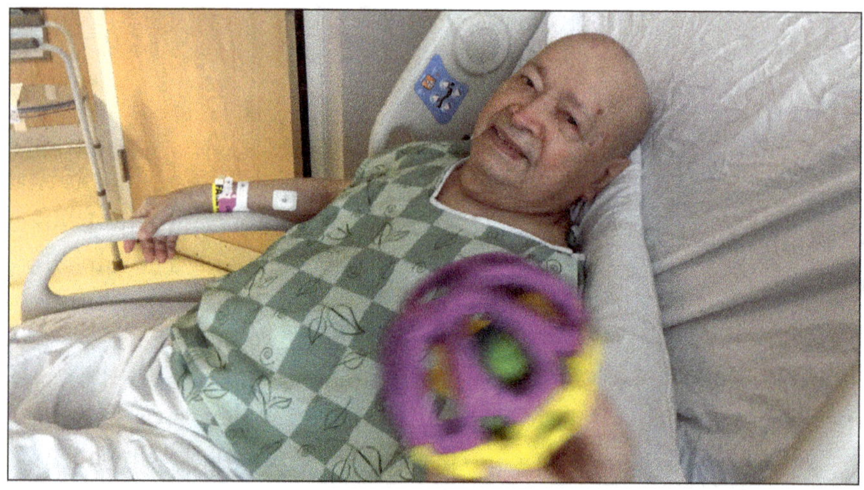

Papi plays with his toys while in the hospital.

So many shifts and changes of staff. When he is not being pricked or poked Papi has a great time. Each new person that comes he believes is there to visit him. They ask me his name, but I tell them to ask him.

"What is your name?"

Papi's chest swells. He is proud to say, "Me llamo José Ramón Peña Hernández de Humacao."

I have a simple conversation with my father in front of the staff, so they can see it can be done, and that he enjoys it. All other questions by the staff are aimed at me.

He has all sorts of tests done. They are all inconclusive. He is given

Valium so they can try doing another MRI, but he is totally alert. He can not cooperate, so it is unsuccessful.

The staff take turns squeezing Papi's abdomen here and there. "¿Duele?" (Does this hurt?)

He responds "No," every time. He doesn't even flinch. They decide to do an abdominal ultrasound. The results show a dilated bile duct with stones, surprising everyone! How can he not be in excruciating pain?

An infectious disease specialist is consulted, then a Gastroenterologist. Papi undergoes an Endoscopic Retrograde Cholangiopancreatography (ERCP), removing a large amount of stone, debris and sludge from the duct but not fully clearing the duct due to its large diameter. A stent is put in place. I'm given instructions to see another Gastro specialist at the uptown Charlotte hospital to complete the procedure. This is to be done within two months.

I'm so glad they found the source of Papi's problem, and it is being dealt with. I still can't believe he is not in pain … but I'm so *very, very grateful!*

04/15/19 CUSHION AS HAT

As you already know, Papi loves hats. He loves handling them as well as wearing them. Today he sits in a chair in his room next to his recliner. He notices a seat cushion on the recliner and decides it would make a great hat!

He puts it on top of the Panama hat he was wearing. He makes me chuckle! Always creative, *never self-conscious.*

What a wonderful state of being.

04/30/19 Papi's Birthday

Today Papi turns 93! Joey and Rae came from Puerto Rico to celebrate. We go to Papi's birthday party at the elderly home. It consists of cutting the birthday cake after lunch. The dining room has been decorated by Manuel. Very festive. Papi wears the large birthday hat again. I love that funny hat.

We take lots of pictures. We sing the Happy Birthday song and Papi sings too. When it ends, we all clap, including Papi.

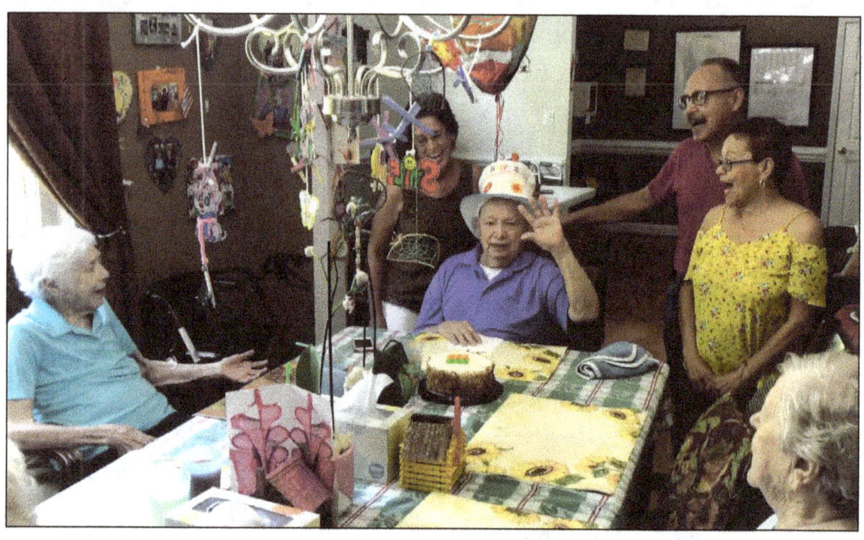

Papi's 93rd birthday party.

My brother begins to sing the Puerto Rican birthday song, "Felíz en tú Dia."[17] Rae joins him. It expresses friendly birthday blessings, filled with peace and a desire for many more birthdays.

Papi looks up with wonder at Joey during the entire song. I observe the beautiful moment. Then we all eat cake. Papi loves the cake.

Afterwards Papi opens the presents. I had brought him a new activity toy. He doesn't know quite what to do with it yet. Joey has brought him a new straw hat. Papi knows *exactly* what to do with it. He puts it on his head. A happy celebration!

---

[17] "Felíz en tu Dia" by Puerto Rican songwriter Emilio Alberto Aragón Bermúdez

05/01/19 Scheduler for ERCP

Papi has been referred to the best surgeon in the area to complete the ERCP procedure. The surgeon needs to meet Papi before the procedure can be scheduled, so I bring Papi from south Waxhaw to Charlotte. I hope he doesn't have an accident in his Depends. Papi, as usual, doesn't know where he is or who he is meeting. He's just happy to be on an outing and meeting new people.

He sings in the waiting area. Other waiting patients smile as they listen. The meeting with the surgeon goes well. Papi is smiling and happy: "Yo soy José Ramón Peña Hernández."

The doctor says, "Let's schedule it."

We follow the scheduler to her office, where we sit across from her. She gets on her computer and researches a date for the ERCP. A few minutes later she announces a date three-and-a-half months from now. I tell her the surgeon at the hospital said my father needed the procedure done within two months. She looks at me and says, with definite finality, that there are no openings before three-and-a-half months and there's nothing she can do. I say that at his age, and with the condition of his bile duct, it should not be put off. She reiterates there's nothing she can do.

Papi, who has been sitting quietly this entire time, humbly speaks up. "Ya no entiendo las cosas muy bien, pero si me lo explican, yo trato de ayudar."

I translate for her: "I don't understand things as well as I used to, but if you explain, I'll try my best to help."

She stares at Papi, transfixed. Her face changes. It loses its toughness. She is affected. She stands up and asks us to please stay seated for a few minutes. Then she leaves the room.

She returns about five minutes later. She is all smiles and announces that she was able to get Papi an appointment in six weeks!

She says to me, "Your father is precious. Your father is just precious." *Papi won her over.* Nothing *I* did. *He did it.*

He didn't have an accident today.

05/08/19 By the Fountain

Papi sits by the fountain, very talkative today. He and Manuel have a conversation about the water. Papi says, "¿Quieres mojarte? (Want to get wet?) He chuckles and points to the fountain. Making a circling motion with his hand he adds, "Ahí. Camina alrededor." (There. Walk around it.)

Manuel asks, "¿Está fría el agua, Don Joe?" (Is the water cold, Don Joe?)

"Sí. Todo el tiempo." (Yes. All the time.) "Uno viene aquí a oír esto." (One comes here to hear this.) He is referring to the sound of the water in the fountain.

He gets up. Moving well today, he walks over to the fountain without his walker and puts his hand up to feel the water flowing from the third tier. He walks around the fountain and sits back down. He not only talks the talk, he walks the walk. He knows exactly how to demonstrate what he says.

My **smart** *little boy!*

05/13/19 and 05/24/19

Papi is still leading walks around the house.
You go, Papi!

05/30/19 Red Ball, Birds & Mirror

We're together in Papi's room. He sits in his recliner. The "red ball" still catches his eye and he points to it saying, "Mira eso. Colorado."

Then he stands up and walks to the edge of his bed so he can look at the birds feeding outside his window. Fascinated.

He gets up, and I do too. He sees our reflection in the mirror which hangs on the wall, and points to it. "Mira eso." I snap a picture.

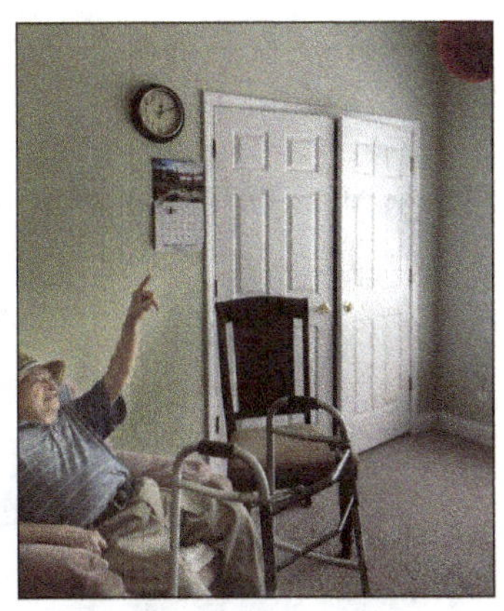

Papi points at the red ball.

Look at that!

I sure love my *little boy!* I sure enjoy being with him and seeing everything through his young eyes.

06/12/19 ACTIVITY MITTEN

A friend from the North Mecklenburg Community Chorus made an Activity Mitten for Papi. So nice of her! I take it to Papi and he spends time examining and handling the tiny trinkets that are knitted into the mitten. A rubbery bracelet, a small pink pom pom

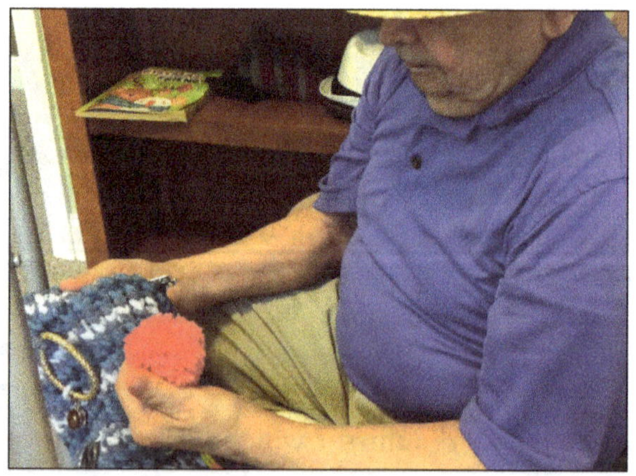

Papi with his activity mitten.

(the type you see at the top of children's hats), a Carolina Panthers NFL football blue charm on a gold bracelet. He talks about it as he handles each trinket.

"¿Qué es esto aquí?" (What is this here?)

"Aquí está. Por aquí." (Here it is. Around here.)

"Ahí, ahí, ahí." (Here, here, here.)

"Así, así, así." (Like this, like this, like this.)

"Le doy la vuelta." (I turn it around.)

06/19/19 Paddle Ball

Papi can play paddle ball. His coordination is quite good! I'm impressed.

06/23/19 Picnic at Cane Creek Park

Another picnic at Cane Creek Park on a beautiful day. The whole gang is enjoying the outdoors.

Doesn't Papi look happy?

06/24/19 No Pain After ERCP

Papi has just undergone the second ERCP to finish cleaning out the bile duct. The surgeon afterwards talks to me about how it went. He explains that there was so much sludge and stones in the duct that if they had not emptied it, it would soon have been blocked and it would have been fatal!

Internally I thank God that Papi influenced the scheduler so that the procedure hadn't been scheduled another two months from now!

Then the surgeon goes on to explain that my father will not be in any more pain. I told him that Papi had *never complained* of pain. He looks at me incredulously, as if it couldn't be possible. I explain that it took three hospital stays before the doctors found what was wrong with him. That they had poked and prodded, poked and prodded, asking if it hurt and he always said "No." That he never even flinched. What pain?

I cannot begin to express how grateful I am that Papi did not feel the pain he should have been in!

So many things fell into place so that Papi could continue to live. God has made it very clear that it is not yet time for Papi's homecoming.

I'm in awe of it all.

06/26/19 HELP ME!

Two days after Papi had the ERCP he is back in the hospital. His stomach is distended. He has developed a Small Bowel Obstruction (SBO). The backup of stomach fluid needs to be emptied. In order to do this *a tube needs to be inserted through his nose down to his stomach.*

They say he will need to swallow. I tell them that he will not understand what they want him to do. There are four people. Two people hold his arms, the third to insert the tube, and the fourth is Hispanic to explain what they are doing. I say he will not understand. He doesn't even know that he is in a hospital and that they are hospital staff. He thinks they are new friends that have come to visit him!

They begin. Papi screams, "¡Ay! Duele. ¡Ayúdenme!" (Ow! Hurts. Help Me!) They tell him to swallow. He keeps screaming. They continue trying. He continues screaming that he's in pain and to please help him. This goes on for about *20 excruciating minutes.* It is heart wrenching for me.

They finally give up and remove the tube, at which Papi immediately looks at them and says, "¡Gracias! ¡Gracias por ayudarme y salvándome!"

The Hispanic translator's mouth drops. I translate: "Thank you. Thank you for helping me and saving me!" Everyone is silent. Stunned. Now it is *they* who are trying to understand.

My heart is pierced at knowing my father never thinks ill of anyone anymore, so he does not even realize it is his "saviors" who were inflicting his pain.

Later the hospital sends their expert to try. This time I wait outside the room. In less than five minutes it is done. He is on the way to recovery. Within a couple of days his bowels start to work on their own.

No surgery needed.

He is sent home.

08/02/19 ASPIRATING

Papi has crackling in his lungs. Not swallowing well. He is sent to the ER and ends up admitted to the hospital again. I'm with him 24/7. They perform various tests. When doing a swallow test they find that solids go down, and that liquids go down but then come back up. This can end up in his lungs (aspiration) which in turn can cause pneumonia.

I know from experience that this is not a good thing. This is how I lost my mother seven years ago: fluid in her lungs.

After five days Papi is sent home with antibiotics, meds to heal his esophagus, and instructions to mix a thickener into all his liquids.

08/11/19 SQUEEZING BALL

Manuel sends me a video. In it, he gives Papi a tennis ball. He says, "Apachurrala." Papi laughs a nervous laugh. He doesn't understand what Manuel is asking of him. *I* don't understand what Manuel is asking of him. I think to myself that Manuel is probably using a Mexican slang word that Puerto Ricans don't use.

After Manuel says "Apachurrala" a couple of times Papi puts the ball down.

Manuel changes his instructions and says, "*Aprietela. Apriete la* pelota. *Apriete la* pelota así." (*Squeeze* it. *Squeeze* the ball. *Squeeze* the ball like

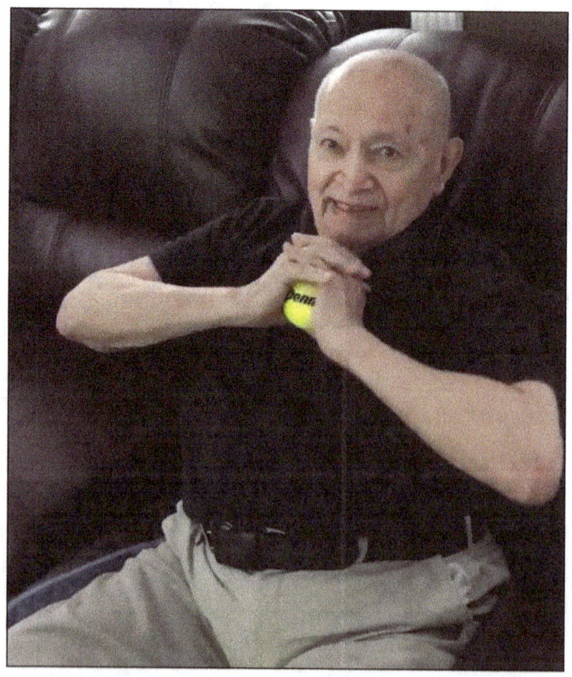

Papi squeezes the ball.

this.) He demonstrates what he wants Papi to do.

Now Manuel is talking Papi's language! Papi immediately picks up the ball, puts it between his palms, interlocks his fingers and squeezes.

Manuel then asks, "¿Está la pelota dura o blandita?" (Is the ball hard or soft?')

Papi squeezes the ball again. He squeezes hard, squinting his eyes with effort, and says, "Dura. Blandita no se ve." (Hard. Doesn't appear soft.)

"¿Cómo te sientes, Don Joe?" (How do you feel, Don Joe?')

"Yo me siento bastante bien." (I feel pretty good.)

"Que bueno." (That's good.)

08/15/19 No-Pain Appendicitis

Manuel informs me that Papi has had diarrhea for *four* days. He thinks it might be C-Diff (clostridioides difficile), which can be fatal. I take Papi to a dedicated ER, with no hospital.

I've done some research and I think the diarrhea is due to the thickener in his liquids that he was put on after last week's hospital stay. The thickener is dextrin, which is usually used to add fiber to diets to obtain regularity. Papi has always been regular, but since August 7 has been taking dextrin in liquids at least eight times a day. I know, because I've seen him at breakfast drinking three eight-ounce glasses of liquid: one of water, one of juice and one of milk. Then at lunch, one of juice and one of water. The same at dinner. Then another glass of water during the day. So of course he now has diarrhea.

At the ER I tell the doctor this, but he still puts my father through tests. I'm so frustrated they aren't listening to me. A little later the doctor comes to discuss the results of an ultrasound/imaging test and says my father's appendix is so inflamed he needs surgery right away!

How can this be? My father hasn't complained of pain. Again, he's been poked and prodded, poked and prodded, again and again and he doesn't even flinch. When asked if it hurts, he says, "No."

How can this be? This is August. In June his appendix was fine.

Yes, do the surgery.

I'm confused, I pray, then I see.

When Papi was in the hospital August 2 through August 7, I really hadn't wanted to be there. After Papi's UTIs had finally cleared, *and* he had the ERCP procedure, I thought Papi would be well for a while. I was terribly disappointed when he ended up in the ER again on August 2. My whole life stopped *again*. I canceled out of things and commitments I wanted to keep. I felt, *Really, again? What now?*

I was with Papi in the hospital 24/7 again. Looking out for him, making sure he didn't hurt himself and making sure the hospital staff took proper care of him. The August 2-7 ordeal was especially difficult for me because it was the *first time* in all of Papi's hospital stays that I didn't want to be there. I wanted *my* life back.

But now I pondered: God provided early retirement for me so I could be there for Papi. I had known this in my head.

Now, I embraced it in my heart. I was glad, again, to be there for Papi. Now, it was not only something I said or thought. It became my heart's reality.

Now that I was in the ER again with Papi I had total peace. I'd had no peace August 2-7, but experienced total peace now.

God used the August 2-7 hospital stay:

- so it could be found that he aspirated;
- so that he was put on a thickener;
- so Papi would have diarrhea;
- so his inflamed appendix could be found;
- so the appendix could be removed *before* it burst;
- so *Papi would not die.*

God spared his life because Papi's life is worth living … still.

08/16/19 FINDING A SURGEON

The ER can't find a surgeon that will perform Papi's appendectomy! Not in *any* of the hospitals he's been in! *Nobody wants to touch him at 93 years old with Alzheimer's!*

Internally I ask, *Why do his age and condition matter? He is still a human being!*

They recommend Atrium Union. I say, "Sure, *anywhere* you can find a surgeon that will operate on Papi."

At this hospital they find a surgeon who is willing. He is African American.

He is willing to perform surgery on my father, and Papi is transferred to the hospital.

After the surgery the surgeon tells me that Papi will be fine. He declares that although Papi is 93 years old, he has the strong body of a 63-year-old and should heal well.

I bless this man! God bless him!

08/17/19 Bésame Mucho in Ukrainian

The hospital staff at Atrium Union are amazing with Papi during his stay there.

A young nurse comes to tend him, smiling and speaking sweetly with a heavy Ukrainian accent. My father is happy to have a visitor, and such a nice one. He immediately starts to sing for her. "Bésame, Bésame mucho…"

She smiles and says to him, "I know that song. I know it in my language. Ukrainian."

She sings a duet with him. Singing the same song. Papi in Spanish, she in Ukrainian.

A beautiful duet.

I had no idea that this great Spanish classic was sung in different languages all over the world. I'm amazed.

Hearing the duet wraps me in a warmth that's indescribable.

I bless this hospital and their staff. People with heart!

08/18/19 Coban

During this, Papi's fourth hospital stay, I find that if I put Coban compression bandage rolls in each of his hands he stops picking at his IV. He also stops picking at his head.

When he drops one, I put it back in his hands and he is distracted again. It is squishy. He has a good hard grip. He squeezes them and it satisfies his desire to do something with his hands.

He goes to scratch his head and I put Coban in each of his hands.

He brings his hands together, putting the two Coban rolls together, end to end.

He puts his finger inside the hole in one of them and looks at his finger coming out the other end. Then wiggles his finger. My **cute** *little boy!*

He puts one of them up to his eye and looks across the room. A telescope. He points at the things he sees through it. My **creative** *little boy!*

He puts one to his mouth and blows it like a bugle. Tatarata!

Ha. Ha. He is having fun. He doesn't hurt himself. He plays with the Coban rolls for a long time.

Till he falls asleep, holding them.

08/21/19 Drive Home, Demos Gracias

After Papi's hospital stay I drive him home. He has done well and was discharged with a lot of optimism on the part of the surgeon. I am grateful and a "corito" (a Spanish church song) bubbles up in me. I sing "Demos Gracias al Señor"[18] ("Let's Give Thanks to the Lord") out loud.

I sing the first of four verses. Papi starts to sing the chorus with me and continues to sing *each* chorus with me. Each verse follows a part of the day. In the morning birds sing praise, in the afternoon flowers sing praise, in the evening stars sing praise and at *all* times mankind sings praise to the Lord. The chorus entreats us to also give our thanks to the Lord!

Papi not only brings joy to those around him…

He brings joy to me because he is…

My **joyful** *little boy!*

08/30/19 Nancita

When I first let someone know that my dad has advanced Alzheimer's, most of the time they ask if he still recognizes me. I tell them I *never* wait for him to recognize me.

The one time I *did* wait he looked at me as if he were trying to place me and said, "Yo cómo que te conozco." (I think I know you.)

---

[18] "Demos Gracias al Señor" by Spanish Priest songwriter Cesáreo Gabaráin.

I think I know you!

I could tell he was trying to remember and was uncomfortable. Why put him through that? He can not give me what is no longer in his brain to retrieve. Instead, I do what my brother Joey taught me to do. I greet him with a smile and identify myself right away.

"Hola Papi. Soy tú hija, Nancy." (Hello Papi. I'm your daughter, Nancy.)

His face lights up. "O Nancita. Nancita *mi hija*." (Oh Nancita. Nancita, *my daughter*.)

Now I know *he knows* who I am.

Nobody else in my entire life has called me that.

He is the *only* person who has ever called me "Nancita."

09/04/19 STAPLES REMOVED

Papi has come through having his appendix removed … and parts of his large and small intestines too.

The surgeon had to remove parts of the intestines because they did not look good. He took out all that looked bad. The biopsy results confirmed no parts were malignant!

Gracias a Dios!

Today I take Papi to have his multiple stitches removed. Papi has a high tolerance for pain, so I'm not too worried. Papi is lying on his back and the surgeon begins picking the staples out. Papi says, "Eso duele." (That hurts.) He feels it!

I quickly hold his hands and get near his face, his ears, saying it will be over soon. He winces. It hurts me too, in my heart. Nobody exists except Dad to me. I sing "Son de la Loma," one of his favorite songs. He doesn't sing. It's the first time he *doesn't* sing when he hears it. But he smiles. He smiles! The doctor makes haste, and then it is over.

My **brave** *little boy!*

Papi's Life Continues

09/19/19 Buttoning his own Shirt

Papi likes to explore with his fingers. He likes feeling textures and trying to figure things out. Today he can't wait to show me what he's learned. He looks at me and points his right index finger as if to say, "Pay attention to what I'm about to show you."

He is wearing a shirt with three buttons near the collar. He can't see what he's doing, but he is feeling it. Using only one hand, his left hand, he unbuttons the shirt slowly. Then he sits looking at me, smiling, so proud of himself.

I say, "Wow, Papi. Muy bien hecho." (Wow, Daddy. Well done.) Then he points his index finger in the air again, so I pay attention. Using only his left hand again he slowly takes the second button and puts it in the first hole. I *don't* correct him. Then he finds the third button and puts it in the second hole. He sits and smiles. He's done. The shirt is not buttoned perfectly, but it *is* buttoned.

I say, "Perfecto, Papi. Estoy muy impresionada contigo." (Perfect, Daddy. I'm so proud of you.) He is beaming! My *smart* little boy!

Papi buttons his shirt by himself.

09/22/19

Papi sitting in the rear screened in porch, getting fresh air.

10/01/19 Keys

Manuel has created a piggy bank using a large plastic coffee container. The black lid has a slit. Manuel gives Papi another container full of colored keys. He has taught Papi what to do with the keys. Papi takes one key at a time and puts them in the slot!

There are quite a few to do. What a great way to keep busy.

My *industrious little boy!*

Papi puts the keys in the slot on the lid.

10/12/19 Time at the Fountain

I sit with Papi by the fountain in front of his house. He is play-ing with a new toy. It's a maze puzzle with a little ball. Papi turns

"Look how it moves."

it this way and that, saying, "Mira cómo se mueve." (Look how it moves.)

The ball gets stuck, and he has trou-ble moving it from its spot so he smacks the maze on the side to dislodge it. Ha!

I help him a little, so the balls start to move about again. He continues to move the maze this way and that, and the ball moves this way and that.

He continues to say, "Mira cómo se mueve."

He starts to move his feet. He likes the sound of the gravelly rocks under his feet. He looks at his feet and moves them, this way and that. Forward and back. Crunch, crunch, crunch.

Then he puts the maze down and points in the air. He

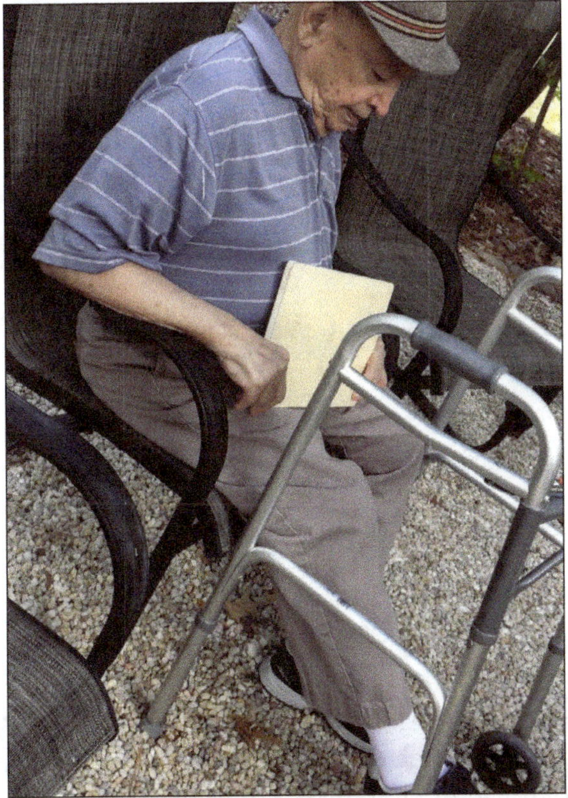

Crunch, crunch, crunch.

points at the birds as they chirp and fly. He looks at the fountain, attracted by the sound of the gurgling water.

I start singing "Inolvidable" (Unforgettable) and he continues the song, so I stop and let him sing. He sings the entire song.

I start singing "Bésame Mucho" and he sings the whole song. I love to hear him. He still sings on key, on pitch.

Then he sings "Quizás." I love it.

He holds a yellow Easter egg that Manuel has put in his hand. He examines it. Feels it. Lifts it. Then he hears a car go by and stops and turns his head toward the road so he can see it. He is so alert. Nothing wrong with *his* ears.

10/28/19 Popping His Lips

Papi sits with a light in his eyes, popping his lips. Just like a child when he first discovers he can make sounds with his mouth. He purses his lips and blows air out, popping his lips. First slowly, then faster. He thinks it's the greatest thing. I giggle.

11/19/19 Pedicures and Toe Nail

Papi has been getting his toenails cut by a nail service about every three months. Today Manuel let me know that Papi's little right toe nail came off.

There is no pain or bleeding.

11/26/19 Making Christmas Ornaments

Today at Papi's elderly home, each resident crafts a "snowman" as a Christmas ornament. They had received two or three round pieces of wood that had been glued together as the body, with twigs for arms.

They add eyes and buttons with a marker. Then they paste green felt gloves and a red hat and scarf on their snowmen.

All need different degrees of help; Lilly the least, Papi the most. He can't remember how to hold the marker for writing. Manuel shows him, but Papi can't copy what Manuel did. Papi just holds it. I put the marker in Papi's hand in the writing position, but he keeps shifting it to a holding position. I decide to hold his hand with the marker and, with difficulty, we draw the eyes and buttons together.

Then Manuel puts glue on the ends of the twigs and asks Papi to pick up the green gloves and put them on the glue. Papi doesn't pick the gloves up. Instead, he presses down on the green felt gloves, right where they are. He looks happy. He thinks he is doing exactly what was asked of him.

Then Manuel asks Papi to give him the gloves. Papi picks the gloves right up and hands them to Manuel. Manuel pastes the gloves, hat and scarf on the wooden snowman, while Papi watches.

Voilà! All done.

After crafts we all sit down in the living room and watch a DVD of an old *Lawrence Welk Show*. Lots of singing and dancing on the show. All the residents, including Papi, clap when a song and/or dance finish, so I do too. At one point Papi begins singing "Son de la Loma." He sings the whole song. I guess he wanted to join in the singing too.

After a while Papi looks up at me and asks, "¿Quien eres tú?" (Who are you?)

"Soy tú hija Nancy." (I'm your daughter Nancy.)

"Nancita."

At this point in his life he may not recognize me, but when he hears my name, he knows.

"¿Dónde tú vives?" (Where do you live?)

"En Carolina del Norte." (In North Carolina.)

We still go through this routine even after two-plus years. He doesn't know where *he* lives. I believe he thinks he's still in Puerto Rico.

That's okay.

I'll never say anything to him about it. Don't want to confuse him.

He's happy!

That is all that matters.

I'm happy!

12/01/19 Hanging Christmas Ornaments

Hanging ornaments on the Christmas tree.

I arrive to see the Christmas tree is up and everyone is busy hanging ornaments on the tree. Manuel hands Papi an ornament and Papi gingerly attempts to put it on the tree. He releases it, and it falls. He doesn't know how to hang it, so Manuel assists him. Papi hangs three ornaments.

I notice the wooden snowmen ornaments they made are hanging on the tree too. See one?

12/09/19 Sleepyhead

I go to visit Papi today from 11:30 a.m. till 12:30 p.m. He sleeps most of the time I'm there. Manuel explains, saying, "Don Joe was up all night fidgeting with the blinds by his bed!"

So … that's why he couldn't stay awake.

Well, when lunch is announced, he wakes up just fine. I leave him heartily eating!

LOL!!!

2019 Christmas Season

12/23/19

It's Christmastime. My loving husband Tommy and I perform again for Papi's elderly home. The residents are engaged, but not as much as last year. One sings, but nobody dances or even stands. Papi sways to the music with his eyes closed, as if in a rapture. Many smiles.

That same evening, Papi is unresponsive and running a fever. He is sent to the ER in Atrium Union in Monroe where they find E-Coli in the blood. Septic. He is put on a long round of IV antibiotics.

12/24/19

As usual I'm staying with Papi 24/7. Tommy comes by with some food. Papi is doing better. He's alert.

When I'm in the hospital with Papi, I'm not able to brush Papi's teeth like Manuel does. If I try, Papi clamps his jaw down on the toothbrush. He doesn't understand what I'm trying to do. He only understands when Manuel does it.

So instead, after Papi eats, I give him some water. He automatically swishes it around in his mouth. One cheek puffing, then the other, one cheek puffing, then the other. Then he swallows the water. It's better than nothing! This is how Papi cleans his mouth while in the hospital.

12/25/19

Merry Christmas from Atrium Union Hospital!

Papi's fever finally breaks. One of the RNs, Rosa, comes by as Papi is waking up and wishes him "¡Felíz Navidad!" so he begins to sing the song written by José Feliciano, which is world famous. The nurse and technician are both impressed. My daddy is back!

He sings "Felíz Navidad" to everyone who comes today.

I take a short break with my loving son who takes me out to eat at a local restaurant for Christmas.

12/26/19

It's decided that the IV antibiotics are working. The septic culture is no longer growing. Still, Papi will need the IV for at least another week.

Tommy has been home caring for our dogs. He lets me know he thinks we're losing Abby, my Yorkie. She is 13 years old, has kidney disease, and has stopped eating. Hasn't taken a bite in over two days. She's either mopey because her "mommy" isn't around, or it's her time.

I make a hard decision to go home to care of her. I talk to the doctor and the nurses. I explain. I leave. I leave Papi in their hands and pray. I cry and pray all the way home. For Papi and for my baby, Abby.

I hand feed her, one morsel at a time. She eats! Eats three-quarters of a serving! I take her to the back yard and walk slowly alongside her. She pees. I kiss and coddle her. Sooner than I'd like, I have to leave. Later my husband calls with the good news that she pooped!

I was gone from the hospital for about three-and-a-half hours. When I get back to the hospital the staff say Papi did well. I see that he is feeding himself! He never missed me.

I bless the hospital staff!

12/27/19

Tommy calls me, excited. Abby came to him begging for food. She ate like a big girl.

(My sweet Abby goes on to live another happy year. A full 14-and-a-half years. Thank God!)

12/28/19

It is decided that Papi can go home as long as someone brings him back daily for an IV. He is taken to put a PICC IV on his inner upper arm so that it will be easier to administer the IVs. The procedure is done in a sterile environment. I'm not allowed to go with him. They assure me they will give him a local anesthetic and he will feel no pain. I wait outside. About 20 minutes later it's done. They say he did well.

About 10 or 15 minutes later we get back to his room, where I ask him how he is feeling. "¿Cómo te sientes Papi? ¿Bien?"

He responds, "Me asusté un poquito." (I was a little afraid.)

Wow! He remembers! He remembers! He saw what they did. The entire procedure. It alarmed him. It scared him.

My **brave** *little boy!*

12/29/19

Every time Papi goes to the hospital he stays five to seven days. Regardless of whether he is back to baseline by day two. His routine is interrupted. This means after a while he doesn't walk, he doesn't go to the restroom, he doesn't get a bath standing up, he doesn't get his clothes changed, no exercise, no play time, no mind games. He eats mostly in bed. He is poked and prodded all the time. For his vitals, for his blood, at all times, all the time. I see him change and adjust. He regresses.

This time he isn't interested in getting out of bed. He needs lots of help from the staff to sit up on the recliner. He mostly shows no interest in eating. I have to *spoon* feed him. This is not good for him. It seems like he gives up to this new arrangement, in which he has no control, and no say. In this place, where there is no Manuel.

I never tell Papi we are going home till I have the discharge papers in hand. Today, as soon as it happened, I say to him, "Papi vamos para casa. ¿Esta bien?" (We're going home, Daddy. Is that okay?)

The look on his face shows a little desperation: "Vamos a tratar!" (Let's try!)

Wow. Does he feel like a prisoner? In this place where he has no say in what is done to him? Where he has no say if he can leave? I've been here with him all the time. Does he think that I also am a prisoner with him? To him, do I have no say as well?

We are back at Papi's elderly home. Papi is still weak. First thing Manuel does is take him to the bathroom where he can use the potty. Then he brings him to the dining room and sets a large salad with meat in front of him. Papi *picks up his fork and feeds himself!* I sit next to him and observe. He is already acting more himself. *He eats heartily.* Suddenly he stops, looks at me and says, "Es difícil." (It's difficult.)

Wow, he blows me away. I respond, "Si Papi. Algunas veces es difícil." (Yes Daddy. Sometimes it's difficult.)

01/01/20

When Papi was released, it was on the condition that he return daily for three days for IV antibiotics. I take him to the Atrium out-patient center for the IV. I do this December 30, 2019 through January 1, 2020.

Happy New Year!

01/06/20

I take Papi to Dr. Snaidecki for a follow up appointment. The blood work results show Papi's blood is clear. Praise God!

I can breathe!

My Fascinating Papi and Joey Visits Again

01/09/20

Today my brother Joey and I talk on the phone. I let him know Papi has been in the hospital again, over the holidays. Joey says he doesn't want me to feel alone in my care for Papi. He understands what that's like. Says that if Papi has to be admitted to the hospital again, he will fly to North Carolina from Puerto Rico to stay with him. I'm so grateful to have such a wonderful, supportive brother … but I know I won't take him up on it.

In 2019 I spent a total 40 days in the hospital with Papi. I usually won't let Joey know Papi is in the hospital till *after* Papi is back home. I don't want my brother to worry about Papi. I have this. I have him. In Puerto Rico, Joey took such good care of Mami and Papi. All by himself. I want to give him a proper break from his years of care for them. He has been an amazing son.

02/02/20 Equestrian Shows

Manuel says Papi likes to watch equestrian shows on the Cowboy Channel. That he loves to see the horses jump. Manuel sends me a video.

Papi sits in his room watching television. Manuel is with him. Manuel asks, "¿Ves cómo se llama esa muchacha? Esa." (You see what that girl's name is? That one?) "Comecara."

Papi *laughs*, "Sí, hombre. ¡Ay, señor!" (Yes, man. Lord have mercy!)

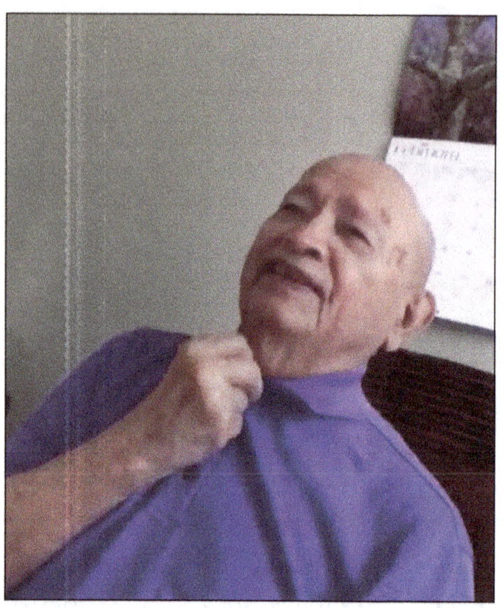

"¡Yupa!"

Papi continues, "Tengo que averiguar eso. Me pongo a verlo ahora. Mira, mira, mira… ¡yupa! ¿Qué es eso? Se viro. Mira eso. ¡Brinco!" (I have to check this out. I'm looking at it now. Look, look, look… ¡yupa! What was that? Took a turn. Look at that. Jumped!)

Manuel asks, "¿Tú puedes hacer eso Joe?" (Can you do that Joe?)

Papi responds, "Yo creo que no." (I don't think so.)

Manuel: "Yo no, tampoco." (Neither can I.)

Papi: "Yo tampoco. Creo que es un poquito fuerte." (Me neither. I think it's a little tough.)

What an awesome life Papi has!

02/06/20 STATIONARY BICYCLE

I arrive at Papi's elderly home to find him on the stationary bicycle again. He has just mounted. I don't interrupt. I sit and observe. His caretaker says, "Don Joe, dame una milla." (Give me a mile.) Papi's feet start moving. Papi is so focused he doesn't notice anything around him. He doesn't notice I'm there. He can see his feet while he moves his legs. He keeps his eyes on his feet. Slowly turning the pedals. Right … left … right … left … on and on.

Manuel routinely checks his mileage, and urges him on, "Un poquito mas." (A little more.) When he reaches the mile, "¡Dame *una milla mas!*" (*Give me another mile!*) Round and round go the pedals till he's completed the two miles. That's twice as much as he used to do! Great! He is then seated in his recliner.

I approach him at this time as if just arriving. "Hola, Papi. Bendición.

¿Te gusta el ejercicio?" (Do you like to exercise?)
"Sí."
I say, "Muy bien."

02/13/20 EATING

Manuel sends me a video. Papi is at the table with an oversized bib, eating, chewing.

Manuel asks, "¿Cómo te sientes José?" (How do you feel José?) Papi answers, "Bien."

He also asks, "¿Qué es lo que estás haciendo? (What are you doing?) Papi keeps chewing and does not reply. Manuel asks again, "¿Qué es lo que estás haciendo?"

Papi asks, "¿Qué es lo que estoy haciendo?"

"Sí."

Papi squints his eyes as if pondering, shrugs his shoulders, then with a smile he says, "Lo que puedo." (Whatever I can.)

"As always (the food's) a little (good.)" HA!

Then Manuel asks, "¿Estás comiendo? "(Are you eating?), and Papi responds "Sí."

"¿Esta buena la comida?" (Is the food good?)

Papi looks down at his plate, getting ready to fill his fork again, and responds, "Cómo siempre, un poquito." (As always, a little.)

Observing the way Papi eats, Manuel exclaims, "Sí. ¡Andale pues!" (Yes. Well get to it then!)

02/17/20 My Brother Joey Comes

Joey and Rae come to visit and stay a few days. Joey says he *needs* to see Papi.

Joey, Rae and I go to visit Papi. Papi is doing so well … physically and emotionally. It is apparent that the Alzheimer's has progressed. Papi really does not remember them. This time he doesn't call me Nancita.

But he's happy and well cared for, and that's what matters. Papi is not as engaged as he used to be. But he still loves to sing.

I start to sing "Inolvidable" and Papi sings the entire song on his own. The melody, perfectly, but here and there he changes a few of the lyrics. Yet his new lyrics fit so well that if you didn't know the original lyrics, you'd think they *were* the original lyrics. Ha!

Joey is glad to see Papi doing well. He says the home would be nothing without Manuel, the main caretaker. I agree that Manuel is amazing. That Manuel is living his God-given purpose.

At home in the mornings, my brother and I talk over coffee. He feels bad that I have been in the hospital so much with Papi. I tell him I wouldn't trade the time I've had with Papi, even in the hospital, for anything in the world. I try to explain.

Experiencing life through Papi, and with Papi, has been a precious gift to me.

To see and share Papi's simple faith, joy, and happiness has been priceless.

Even giving up my activities, *my* life.

In many ways these times with Papi have been some of the best moments in my life.

The simplicity of it.

Everything else is put on hold when I am with Papi.

So I get to enjoy Papi's simple world very deeply.

He is such a **good** *little boy*, and we have a loving relationship.

Joey looks at me with comprehension. He says that was the way he also felt at times when he took care of Mami and Papi, and actually misses those times … precious moments!

03/07/20 Dame La Mano Paloma

Today I visit Papi. I bag a lunch and eat with him and the others at the table. He is talkative, happy, and singing. He starts to sing "Dame la Mano Paloma"[19] (Give me your hand Dove), a Puerto Rican children's New Year's song. The lyrics are about asking a dove to give a hand up to its nest since it's alone, to keep it company.

He stops singing. He has a look on his face as if he realized he was singing something naughty.

If you examine the rest of the lyrics, they talk about falling in love with the dove as it flew by one starry night, and the need to give her her first New Year's Day kiss *alone in her cozy nest*. The singer begs to not be kept waiting.

For a children's song I think there's too many double entendres! Even Papi understands that!

---

[19] "Dame la Mano Paloma" by Puerto Rican songwriter Luis Morales Ramos.

Pandemic Lockdown

03/13/20 Coronavirus Disease 2019

The world has gone into lockdown. There is a new virus named Coronavirus Disease 2019 going around. Being dubbed COVID-19. This is what I know about it:

It began in a laboratory in China. It causes respiratory symptoms like a cold or the flu, much like pneumonia. *It is deadly*, and it is spreading throughout the world. A pandemic. People are to stay at home. If you need to go out, wear a mask. The type of mask doctors and nurses use in a hospital. This is because it is highly contagious.

The nature of COVID-19 makes it especially deadly to the elderly, so for now I can't visit Papi in person. I sure hope this doesn't last long.

03/22/20 Colored Keys and Cup

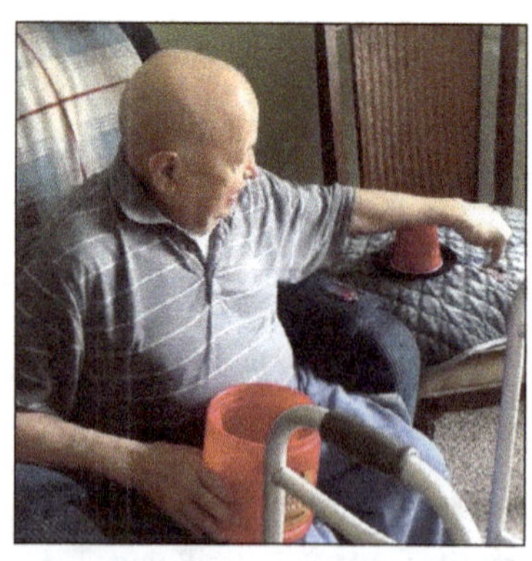

This one.

I can't visit Papi due to the COVID pandemic lockdown, so Manuel sends me a video.

Papi is sitting in his room with the big plastic coffee container on his lap. This time instead of putting the keys through the lid slot, the lid is off and he digs into the container and pulls a gray key out, then lays it on the chair next to him. He pulls a blue key out and lays it next to the gray key. Next is a purple key that he carefully puts on the chair beside the other two keys.

Manuel asks, "¿José, son azules esas llaves?" (José, are the keys blue?)

Papi moves his head up and down and says, "Son azules." (They are blue.) Then he points to the blue key on the chair. "Está aquí." (This one.)

Papi picks up a red plastic cup that was on the chair, looks inside it and puts it back down. Manuel asks, "¿Y ese baso de que color es?" (And what color is that cup?)

Papi picks up the cup and says, "Distinto colores." (Different colors.) Then he holds the cup up to Manuel showing him the inside, which is white, and asks Manuel, "¿De que color?" (What is the color?)

Manuel says, "Por afuera." (On the outside.) Papi keeps looking on the inside of the cup. So Manuel asks, "¿Es rojo por afuera?" (Is it red on the outside?) Then Papi flips the cup over and extends his arm to show him the red side.

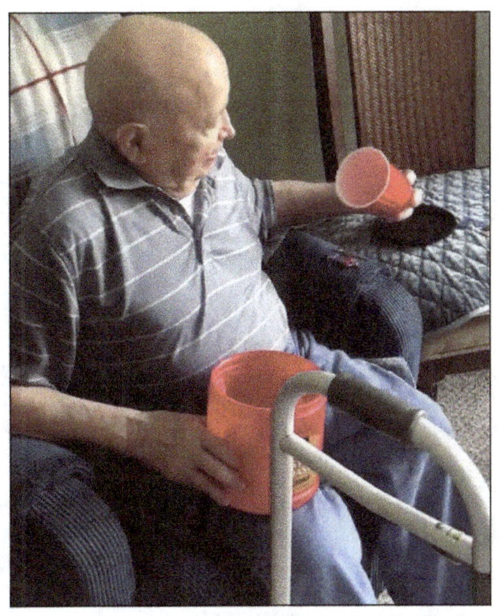

Inspecting the colors.

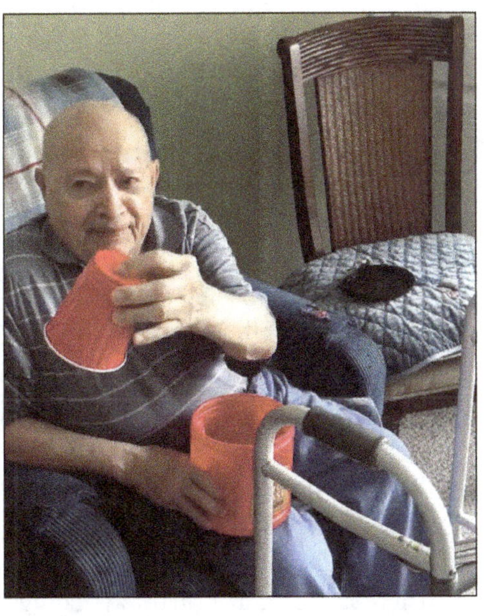

The red side.

04/30/20 Papi's 94th Birthday

Left: Yummy coconut birthday cake.

Right: Claps and sings to himself. Happy 94th!

Today is Papi's 94th birthday!

I still can't visit him due to the COVID pandemic lockdown. I haven't seen him in person since mid-March, but Manuel sends a video.

There is that crazy birthday hat again. I love that hat! They sing the happy birthday song. Papi sings too. When they clap at the end, he claps too.

A coconut birthday cake. *Yum!*

06/06/20 ANOTHER WALK

Hold onto those pants, Papi!

Manuel sends pictures of Papi on another walk around the house. Doesn't he look good for a 94-year-old? He's so fit and trim that he has to stop and let go of his walker to grab hold of his belt, so that his jeans won't fall!

06/17/20 Facetime

Due to COVID restrictions, and for the well-being of all the residents at Papi's elderly home, I just *can't* visit Papi. Manuel lets the residents use his cell phone for Facetime calls. This has made such a difference to me.

This is now how I visit with Papi. I can see that Papi is well and happy.

On these calls Papi sings the following songs, and pieces of other songs too:

"Siempre Alegre" (Always Happy)
"Demos Gracias" (Let's give Thanks)
"Caña Brava" (Wild Sugar Cane) – well, only the "clean" lyrics!
"Son de la Loma" (Song of the Hill)
"Inolvidable" (Unforgettable)
"Bésame Mucho" (Kiss me a lot)

I say, "Papi, tú siempre alegre y contento." (Daddy, you're always happy and content.)

He says, "Hay que buscar cómo hacer las cosas mejor." (You must always look for ways to make things better.)

Papi's words of wisdom.

My **wise** *little boy*!

06/20/20 More Facetime

Another Facetime call today. I Facetime with Papi about once a week. *He doesn't miss me.* He's not *able* to miss me. I Facetime for *me.*

To not only see how he's doing, but to sing with him. To *see him happy* makes *me* happy.

I start singing "Parece que va a llover"[20] (Looks like it's gonna rain).

He sings the next line, then I sing the next, then he sings the next. Back and forth.

The song talks about the sky getting dark then the punchline exclaims to Mother that I'm getting wet.

---

[20] "Parece que va a Llover" by Cuban songwriter Antonio Matas.

He continues:

> Aterriza, que no hay tapón (Land, there is no traffic congestion)
> En la parte del malecón (In the area of the pier)

I start the song again, and we go back and forth taking turns. Sounds just like a call and response song. At least that's how we're singing it.

He continues:

> Aprieta el paso, que nos vamos a mojar (Walk quickly, or we'll get wet)
> Cómo es bonita, yo la quiero conquistar (Since she is pretty, I want to win her over)
> Para que puedan llegar (So that we can arrive)
> Y sigue la loma, y no voy par chalco (And the hill continues, and I don't go to the water hole)
> Y no me voy mojar (And I won't get wet)

I never heard of these lyrics, so afterwards I looked the song up on the internet. Turns out I only knew the chorus, and there are lots of interesting verses. Papi had the music to the verses but was making up most of the lyrics on the fly again.

I sing "Ay, ay, ay, ay" beginning the "Cielito Lindo" song. He sings the rest of the song's chorus.

He starts to sing the "Caña Brava" melody with the following words:

> Pa' mover la caña (To move the sugar cane)
> Cuando tú no puedas (When you can't)
> Cada vez que puedas (Every time you can)

Then he says, "Uno tiene que en la vida poder ir cargando sus cosas. A ver si le salen las cosas bien." (One in life has to carry their own load. To see if things will turn out well.)

More words of wisdom from Papi.

"Bendición Papi." (Bless me father.)

"Dios te guarde." (God protect you.)

07/25/20 Guantanamera

Manuel sends me a video. Papi is sitting at the dining room table. Music plays in the background. The song is "Guantanamera."[21] (Girl from Guantanamo) An old Cuban classic about an old Cuban town. I can hear one of the female residents humming the melody. The one with the beautiful soprano voice.

Papi says, "Mira. Guantanamera. Esa es buena canción. Pa' Guantanamera voy yo." (Look. Guantanamera. That's a good song. To Guantanamera I go.)

Manuel says "Pues Joe, canta la canción." (So, Joe, sing the song.)

Papi laughs heartily.

Papi doesn't wait to be in sync with the music; he starts to sing the chorus: "Guantalamera. Guajira Guantalamera. Guantalameeeraaa. Guajira Guantalamera."

He mispronounces the word; Guantanamera is a girl from Guantanamo, a town in Cuba. Guantala means "hold her." Not sure this means anything, but he mispronounced it.

The verse begins and Papi laughs and says, "Yo no se mas na." (That's all I know.)

---

21   Popular Cuban patriotic song. Lyrics by José Martí, music by Joseíto Fernández

The music gets to the chorus again, and he sings it again, clear and on key, although mispronounced.

He picks at his plate and says "Esto yo creia que era algo, pero no fue así." (I thought this was something, but it wasn't so.) I notice that his plate is empty, so whatever he *did* get he apparently enjoyed!

Manuel asks, "What is the name of the song?"

Papi says, "Guantanamera, pero yo lo único que se es así." (Guantanamera, but all I know is this.) I observe that when he *says* a word he pronounces it correctly, but when he *sings* it, he mispronounces it.

He sings the chorus again. Then he laughs, heartily, and Manuel laughs too. Papi says "Tú te ries. ¡Yo me río también!" (You laugh. I laugh too!) And continues to laugh.

Papi is always so jolly and happy. What a beautiful sound. To hear him laugh the hearty laugh of a child. My **happy** *little boy*!

No Hospital Stay

08/11/20

Papi awoke today lethargic, not walking on his own, and not urinating. A urine sample was taken to Dr. Snaidecki. Late in the day the results show a bad UTI. The doctor gives instructions that Papi be taken to the ER right away.

Manuel recommends the *dedicated* ER in Waxhaw, instead of the crowded *hospital* ER where Papi could be exposed to COVID. Exposure to COVID could be fatal to Papi in his already compromised state. I agree. The hope is that Papi would be treated and sent home. I am very skeptical. Every time Papi has a UTI diagnosis it is *always* followed by a five to seven-day hospital stay. He has *never* been sent home from the ER.

At the ER in Waxhaw, amazingly, Papi has *no wait time* in the waiting room and is immediately put in a room by himself. He is completely lethargic and unresponsive. The doctor says she wants to avoid admitting Papi to the hospital due to COVID. In spite of the fact that they isolate all those with COVID to one hospital wing, COVID is rampant in the hospital. She goes on to say she will start him on IV antibiotics. She wants to see some improvement, some response from him within an hour. If so, she will send him home with oral antibiotics; if not, she will have no choice but to send him to the hospital.

She admits that the norm is to admit him into the hospital because 24 hours is needed for full test results on urine tests, but there is nothing normal about COVID being deadly to compromised elderly. *If* he needs hospitalization, I request they keep him in the current ER until a room is available at the hospital so that he is admitted directly into his room.

I also volunteer to drive him there, as long as I receive assistance moving him when I arrive. The doctor agrees.

She starts him on the drip. I request two Coban rolls to put in his hands, as even when lethargic he seems to be looking for something to grab hold of. I sit and read a book. After about 45 minutes I see Papi is awake and playing with the Coban in his hands! I stand by him so he can see me. He smiles.

"Hola Papi, soy tú hija Nancy."

"Nancita."

I sing, "Parece que va a llover…"

Papi continues and finishes the chorus of the song.

The nurse walks in during this and hears him sing. She runs to tell the doctor. The doctor returns and I tell Papi she has come to hear him sing. He's happy to sing for her. She smiles as she listens to him, and says to me, "I'm sending him home."

Incredible! COVID has definitely changed things. This doctor doesn't want people dying on her watch.

I pray the oral medications work.

08/12/20

Papi begins his oral meds today. Dr. Snaidecki also orders a stronger medication with instructions that they only give it to him after finishing the first medication, and only *if* he starts having symptoms again.

08/21/20

I Facetime Papi. This is the last day of his ER oral meds. He looks and acts fine. His regular jolly self.

08/23/20

Papi has symptoms again and starts on the meds Dr. Snaidecki prescribed. Praying.

09/01/20

Papi finishes the second medication. I Facetime Papi and he looks and acts fine. He's singing. Singing. I pray and wait.

09/10/20

I Facetime with Papi. He looks and acts *great!* Praise God! It's the first time he's had a UTI and was *not* hospitalized!

He sings a lot. "Cielito Lindo," "Son de la Loma," "Demos Gracias al Señor." He changes words at will. Changes the end of "Son de la Loma" to "Al baño, se cayó los niños." (At the bath, the children fell.) It's so silly, I laugh out loud. He really enjoys seeing and hearing me laugh and gives me a broad toothy smile I'll never forget.

He asks, "¿Te gusta cuando canto? La proxima vez canto mas." (You like when I sing? Next time I'll sing more.)

I say, "¡Muy bien! ¡Así es que se canta!" (Very good! That is the way to sing!) So, he starts clapping his hands, as if to say, "When someone sings well, this is how to show appreciation."

So, I start clapping too. I'm still learning from my dad.

After a while he sits back in his recliner, so I say, "Vamos a descansar." (Let's rest.)

He says, "¡Exacto! ¡Si corre pa' riba y pa' bajo no coje na'!" (Exactly! If you run up and down you won't catch anything!) LOL. I just love Papi's words of wisdom.

My landline begins to ring. He hears it and says, "Eso va ligerito." (That goes pretty fast.) LOL.

12/21/20 Teaching Me Improv

Papi has been medicated on and off with Augmentin for recurrent UTIs since August.

Manuel tells me Papi will sluggishly walk and have the shakes, then walk normally with his walker.

Papi goes back and forth like this within the same day.

I Facetime with Papi.

The moment he sees me he says, "¡Tú eres la muchachita que le gusta cantar!" (You're the young girl that likes to sing!)

Wow. I like that reputation! I don't bother telling him I'm his daughter.

"Sí. ¿Cómo estás Papi?"

"Bien."

"¡Bendición!"

"Dios te bendiga."

I start singing songs. Just the beginning or a part of a line here and there; when he sings I let him sing by himself. *Parece que va a llover. Son de la loma. Hay que vivir la vida siempre alegre. Quizás.*

He can still sing melodies perfectly, but he changes the lyrics now about 90 percent of the time. They sort of make sense. They always rhyme.

He sings, we talk, he sings…

Sings to "Quizás:"

"Te estoy esperando, (I'm waiting for you)
Tanto, tanto (So much, so much)
Para que todos vengan (So that all will come)
Aquí siempre, cántando" (Here always, singing)

I ask: "¿Comiendo bien?" (Eating well?)
Papi: "Sí. ¿Porque?" (Yes, why?)
Me: "Te vez bien." (You look well.)
Papi: "*Estoy* bien." (*I am* well.)
To the melody of "Quizás:"

"Que cómo, dónde y cuando (How, where, when)
Y todos preguntando (And all are asking)
Quizás, quizás, quizás" (Perhaps, perhaps, perhaps)

Papi says, "Yo vengo horita, a chequiar (Spanglish word) a ver lo que pueden hacer." (I'll come in a little while, to check, to see what can be done.)

I say, "Ahí viene la Navidad." (Christmas is coming.)

Papi: "Sí, yo tengo que estar pendiente. Me dice lo que hay. Para ir adelante. Ir, y empezar, y seguir." (Yes, and I have to be ready. Tell me what there is. So I can go ahead. Go, and start, and continue.)

He hums "Quizás."

He says, "Vamos a buscar las cosas. Espero que haiga mucho que hacer. Y se aguantan las cosas. Y se hacen." (Let's go get the things. I expect there will be much to do. And things will hold off. And they get done.)

He continues to sing his original lyrics to "Quizás."

> "Estás pasando el tiempo, (You passing the time)
> Vamos a los muchachos (Lets go to the guys)
> Ver lo que viene (To see what will come)
> Y hací se andan los pasos" (And like this we take steps)

I repeat these last few words, *his* words, to the Quizás melody.

He says, "Así es la idea. Tal vez lo coje horita." (That's the idea. Perhaps you'll get it soon.)

He's *teaching me* how to improv. He's the *master* of improv.

He keeps the improv going for a long time.

I listen.

CHRISTMAS 2020 - TOMMY AND NANCY DON'T PERFORM

Tommy and I can't perform our yearly Christmas-with-a-Latin-Flair Concert for Papi's elderly home due to the COVID pandemic lockdown.

I know Papi lives in the moment and can't feel the lack.

But *I* feel it.

12/28/20 ER WAXHAW

Papi is completely lethargic. Not walking or bearing his weight. Not eating or responding. Not urinating. He is sent to Atrium ER Waxhaw. I meet him there.

No fever.

Ultrasound of bladder shows fluid (although he's not urinating).

Urine sample. Catheter extracts about six ounces. Results shows *no* UTI.

Blood work is good. Liver enzymes, good. Kidneys, good.

They find he is a little dehydrated and start him on IV Fluids. (Not sure how he can be dehydrated with all the fluids he drinks daily!) When the bag is empty he perks up and talks and sings. They give him another bag of fluids. I'm told he either had a mini-stroke, or his Alzheimer's is advancing.

The doctor says they can't do anything else for him and wants to release him. I insist he have a bile duct ultrasound (as in the past nothing showed up in the blood work).

Nothing shows up in the ultrasound. The results are good. I'm told if he's admitted to the hospital the only test they can perform is an MRI.

No! This is where *I* draw the line.

I take Papi to his home although nothing has been found or done, except hydrating.

Manuel agrees that it's probably his Alzheimer's advancing.

Year 2021

What do I write regarding 2021? The second COVID year. Papi is slowly shutting down. Not an easy thing for me, but he seems at peace, and this helps me. When I Facetime I talk and sing to him. I sing all the songs he sang for me these past few years. I tell him I love him.

04/30/21

Today Papi turns 95, but no birthday party this time. Papi is totally lethargic. Manuel sends him to the ER in Waxhaw. I meet Papi there. They do all sorts of tests on Papi. I speak with the doctor, who says there is nothing physically wrong with Papi. It is Alzheimer's.

I'm on the phone with my brother Joey. I'm texting with Manuel. What do we do? Just as Manuel tells me to ask the doctor if hospice should be contacted, the doctor makes his recommendation that hospice should be called in. My brother and I agree. Papi goes back to the elder care home, and hospice begins to come and care for him.

05/01/21

Hospice sends someone to evaluate Papi. We talk on the phone. She shares the following experience:

She put the stethoscope on Papi's chest and asked him to breathe in and out. Manuel was in the room observing. She continued to hold the stethoscope to Papi's chest, telling him to breathe in and out.

Manuel stepped up to Papi and told him in Spanish, "¡Don Joe, respira!" (Don Joe, breathe!) Papi let out a long breath. He had been *holding* his breath the whole time, and *she* hadn't noticed. But *Manuel did.*

She tells me that Manuel will welcome the medical hospice nurse who will take Papi's vitals and give medical instruction, but Manuel has refused the home care nurse. I tell her I trust Manuel completely with my father.

I'm amazed that Manuel, having the care of others in the home, did not accept the hospice home care nurse. He really does care for my Papi. Yes, as always, I trust him completely with my daddy.

05/06/21

Eventually I qualify for the COVID vaccine. Today I finally receive the second dose of the vaccine so that I can visit Papi in person.

I have a bad reaction to the vaccine and spend an entire day in bed with a fever, aches, pains and lethargy. It's okay, my Papi is worth it.

05/10/21

I visit Papi and am told that he is not eating regularly. He no longer feeds himself; someone has to spoon feed him. Sometimes he eats, sometimes he doesn't even respond. He is limp and sleeps his days and nights away. I ask if I can try to feed him.

Manuel gives me detailed instructions on how to feed him: Hold his head up, so that when (and if) he swallows he does not aspirate, to ensure the food goes to his stomach instead of his lungs. Observe that he chews and swallows. Be sure his mouth is empty before offering another spoonful. Take my time, don't rush. Be patient.

For me, the rest of the world does not exist. It's only me and my Papi (my Daddy), so I have all the time in the world.

I talk to him. Tell him I'm his daughter Nancy. I say it's time to eat and that I want him to eat. I put a small spoonful to his lips. They part and he receives the nourishment! Chews slowly and swallows. This continues for about 45 minutes. The plateful that Manuel brought me is empty! Papi has eaten well today. I'm so glad.

05/18/21

Sometimes Papi doesn't eat for days. Sometimes he doesn't eat for me. But today he ate well for me again.

Although I get no response from Papi I still continue to talk and sing to him. I give him all the love I have to give.

06/05/21

Last night at 11:30 p.m. Manuel called and left me a voice message saying he believes I should come see Papi. I pick up the message this morning. I am at Papi's side by 9:00 a.m.

It is apparent Papi's transition to his celestial home will be soon. He is lying in his bed. He is skin and bones, in a fetal position, and breathing heavily through his mouth. Manuel teaches me how to keep Papi's mouth from drying out, not with water but with passion fruit juice, dipping a large swab and spreading it inside his mouth and on his lips.

Manuel has been turning Papi every so often, so that he doesn't get bed sores. He goes to turn him and as he does, he sees Papi flinch. I don't notice it, but Manuel does. He says to me that even with his best efforts Papi is feeling discomfort when moved.

He says he is calling the hospice doctor to order a prescription to the pharmacy in Monroe for Tylenol suppositories. It's Saturday and Manuel wastes no time. He proceeds to call and succeeds, then turns to me and says, "I need you to go to the pharmacy right away to pick up the prescription before they close at noon."

I jump in my car on my mission. Manuel will not allow Papi to be in pain if he can help it. I feel so clueless and am thankful for Manuel and his care for Papi.

I come back with the prescription and for the rest of the day Manuel inserts the suppositories into Papi's bottom every four hours without fail. I stay by Papi's side talking to him, telling him I love him, telling him to rest and wetting his lips and mouth. Papi is not showing signs of being in pain. I'm grateful.

06/06/21

6:30 a.m., Papi goes to Glory. He is in the presence of God. Papi is now complete.

Papi left a legacy of songs with me. When I perform, I continue to honor him by singing these beautiful Spanish songs for the public.

I embrace the last line of "Inolvidable" (Unforgettable). I know it will be true for me, about Papi.

He will unforgettably live on … ***in me.***

EPILOGUE

It has been over two years since Papi left this life for eternal life. Shortly after losing Papi, I went through a Grief Share class in a local church with others that were grieving the loss of a loved one. It did me good to talk about Papi. My time with Papi was priceless.

Sometimes I still wish I could step into Papi's world, Alzheimer's and all. Ah, to rest in Papi's world again. I still miss him so much, but I have no regrets. He didn't die because of a bile duct that became impassable, not due to his appendix bursting, not due to a UTI, and not because of COVID-19. Papi died at the ripe old age of 95. I have no regrets.

My brother Joey and Rae *did* return to Puerto Rico. After being stateside for three months Joey returned ahead of Rae to assess the damage to their home. What he found was daunting. The walls cracked, floors a mess, etc. But Joey was up to the task. He worked on fixing the house for another couple of months before Rae joined him.

At first they talked about plans to leave Puerto Rico and live in the states, feeling they could not live through another Hurricane like Maria again … but the island has recovered. The beauty of the island has returned. Not only returned, but "paradise" now is lovelier than it was prior to Hurricane Maria.

I continue to perform the beautiful songs Papi left behind with me. Tommy and I are especially busy during Hispanic Heritage Month, celebrated from mid-September through Mid-October, where along with our smooth jazz and Latin music we shared the Spanish classics. People have embraced these songs. A Hispanic young man thanked me for singing the music of his family and country.

The Public Broadcasting System (PBS) interviewed Tommy and me for a local PBS program, Carolina Impact. The *Charlotte Observer* interviewed us for the newspaper's Carolina Living section. We perform for public venues, and also for Assisted Living, Senior Living, and Senior Centers in the area.

All this because of the lessons I learned with Papi. Life at any age is worth living, and should be well-lived, full of joy and music.